Working with Political Science Research Methods

5th Edition

Sara Miller McCune founded SAGE Publishing in 1965 to support the dissemination of usable knowledge and educate a global community. SAGE publishes more than 1000 journals and over 600 new books each year, spanning a wide range of subject areas. Our growing selection of library products includes archives, data, case studies and video. SAGE remains majority owned by our founder and after her lifetime will become owned by a charitable trust that secures the company's continued independence.

Los Angeles | London | New Delhi | Singapore | Washington DC | Melbourne

Working with Political Science Research Methods

Problems and Exercises

5th Edition

Jason D. Mycoff
University of Delaware

FOR INFORMATION:

CQ Press
An imprint of SAGE Publications, Inc.
2455 Teller Road
Thousand Oaks, California 91320
E-mail: order@sagepub.com

SAGE Publications Ltd.
1 Oliver's Yard
55 City Road
London, EC1Y 1SP
United Kingdom

SAGE Publications India Pvt. Ltd.
B 1/I 1 Mohan Cooperative Industrial Area
Mathura Road, New Delhi 110 044
India

SAGE Publications Asia-Pacific Pte. Ltd.
18 Cross Street #10-10/11/12
China Square Central
Singapore 048423

Printed in the United States of America

Print ISBN: 978-1-5443-3144-7

Library of Congress Control Number: 2019935303

This book is printed on acid-free paper.

SUSTAINABLE FORESTRY INITIATIVE

Certified Chain of Custody
At Least 10% Certified Forest Content
www.sfiprogram.org
SFI-01028

Acquisitions Editor: Scott Greenan
Editorial Assistant: Sam Rosenberg
Production Editor: Tracy Buyan
Copy Editor: Shannon Kelly
Typesetter: Hurix Digital
Proofreader: Sue Schon
Cover Designer: Janet Kiesel
Marketing Manager: Erica DeLuca

19 20 21 22 23 10 9 8 7 6 5 4 3 2 1

CONTENTS

ABOUT THE AUTHOR

Jason D. Mycoff is associate professor of political science and international relations at the University of Delaware. His research is on American political institutions, in particular the U.S. Congress, congressional committees, and parties.

ACKNOWLEDGMENTS

SAGE wishes to thank the following reviewers for their valuable feedback during the development of this book:

Ewa Golebiowska, Wayne State University

Amanda M. Rosen, Webster University

1 INTRODUCTION

Practice Makes Perfect

While most political science courses deal with government, issues, and politics, research methods is an important component of political science training that helps students better understand coursework and has practical applications. Most political arguments raise claims of fact, as when someone says, "We *should* reform Medicare because it will *decrease* health spending." The first part of the statement takes a normative position (something ought to be done), whereas the second makes a factual claim; it states that one thing leads to another, whether or not anyone wants this to be the case. The goal of our textbook, *Political Science Research Methods,* is to show you how those two types of assertions can be separated and how the latter can be demonstrated empirically. The goal of this workbook is to help you apply those skills.

At first sight, achieving these objectives may seem easy. And it is! But it also requires a degree of thought and care. Moreover, the best way to acquire the necessary skills is to practice actively and then practice some more. After all, no sports team would prepare for a game simply by reading a scouting report. But I believe if you make an honest effort, the process of verification can be fascinating as well as informative.

Most of the exercises in this workbook ask you to think before writing. The thought process is typically straightforward and certainly does not require a strong mathematical aptitude. A thorough reading of the text, attention to class notes, and a dose of common sense should be adequate.

Note also that many questions call for judgment and explanation; they do not necessarily have one "correct" answer. Unless a question is based on a straightforward calculation or reading of a table, you will often be asked to think about a possible solution and to defend your choice.

The chapters in this workbook follow the chapters in the main text. That is, there are exercises for each chapter except the first and last. It is important to read the chapter in the text *before* starting to do an assignment. Many questions require you to integrate a chapter's different elements. Hence, you cannot just try to look up something without grasping the subject matter as a whole.

An orderly, step-by-step approach is the best way to work through the exercises in this workbook; it will help you avoid errors and make the important concepts relayed in the text clearer. If you are asked to make any calculations, you should do them neatly on a separate piece of paper that you can, with instructor approval, turn in along with your answers. Here's a tip: Your intermediate calculations or scrap work should be written in such a way that someone can reconstruct your thought processes. Figure 1-1 provides a simple example. It shows that the respondent first clarified the requested information and then performed the computation on a separate sheet of paper.

Figure 1-2 gives an example of someone using the workbook itself as a scratch pad and the ensuing confusion that often comes from sloppy writing and thinking. Note that some of the numbers were copied incorrectly and that the arithmetical operations are out of order. (The correct answer, by the way, is $28,650, not $24,150.)

FIGURE 1-1 ■ Be Organized and Neat

Party	Freq.
Democrat..................	200
Republican	150
Independent	100
None........................	50
Total......................	500

[Separate sheet of paper]

Percent = Number over total times 100.

200 Dems/500 = 2/5 = .4

.4 × 100 = 40%

Refer to the table above.

What percentage of the sample are Democrats?   40%

FIGURE 1-2 ■ Sloppiness Leads to Errors

What is the mean, or average, per capita income of the following six countries? <u>24,150</u>

Luxembourg	$32,700	144,900
United States	31,500	$\dfrac{144{,}900}{\cancel{5}\ \ 6} = 24{,}150$
Bermuda	30,000	
Switzerland	26,400	~~32,500~~ 32,700
Singapore	26,300	31,500
Hong Kong	25,000	3,000
		26,400
		26,300
		~~25,500~~ ~~25,800~~ 25,000
		~~1,~~414,900

All the data you need to do the exercises in this workbook are included in the workbook or textbook or can be downloaded from the student Web site at https://edge.sagepub.com/johnson9e. When you are looking for a specific data set on the student Web site, simply click on the appropriate folder on the site. For instance, if you are looking for the states data set for use with exercises in chapter 11, open the folder called "States Data" and you will find multiple versions of the file in different file formats. Once you learn how to use a program it is easy to explore a variety of hypotheses and problems. Besides being intrinsically interesting, knowledge of research methods provides skills that will help you in other courses and in many professions.

Have fun!

2 THE EMPIRICAL APPROACH TO POLITICAL SCIENCE

In chapter 2 of the textbook, we describe the scientific method and argue that it underlies empirical political science research. We note that empirical claims are sometimes difficult to distinguish from other kinds of statements. Also, it is not always clear whether and how empirical analysis can be applied to propositions stated in theoretical and practical terms. The following questions, problems, and assignments therefore offer opportunities for you to think about the application of the empirical approach. Note that not all of the questions have one "right" answer. Many, in fact, require a lot of careful thought. And it is often necessary to redefine or clarify words or phrases, to look for hidden assumptions, and to consider whether or not statements can be "translated" into scientific terms.

Exercise 2-1. The empirical approach to research involves many technical terms. These terms describe important concepts in the scientific method. Below you will find a number of terms that appear somewhat similar but represent very different concepts. Define each term and explain how they differ.

a. Empirical and nonempirical

_____

_____

b. Normative and nonnormative

_____

_____

c. Induction and deduction

_____

_____

d. Theory and fact

_____

_____

Exercise 2-2. In the space below, define the scientific method by identifying the most important concepts included in the method. Why are these the most important components?

_____

_____

_____

_____

_____

_____

_____

_____

Exercise 2-3.   Chapter 2 mentions several characteristics of scientific knowledge. It also warns about confusing commonsense and casual observations with verified or potentially verifiable claims. In this exercise you will try to identify and differentiate between normative statements, which are statements that suggest how things *should* be, and empirical statements, which are statements that can be measured, tested, or verified through observation. For each of the following statements, decide if the statement is normative, empirical, a combination of the two, or if there is not enough information in the statement for you to decide. Write your responses in the space provided after each statement and briefly explain why you think your answer is correct.

a.   Hillary Clinton won the Catholic vote in the 2016 presidential election.

_____

_____

_____

b.   North Korea should be deterred from continuing to pursue development of a nuclear weapons program.

_____

_____

_____

c.   Early voting periods should be shortened because they disproportionately favor Democratic candidates for office.

_____

_____

_____

d.   Multiparty systems are better for representation than two-party systems.

_____

_____

_____

e. Nevada has a higher proportion of female state legislators than any other state.

_____

_____

_____

f. Senior citizens are more likely to vote than college students.

_____

_____

_____

g. The Brazilian runoff election was close enough that there should have been a recount.

_____

_____

_____

h. Freedom of religion is a fundamental right of all people.

_____

_____

_____

i. Republican presidents are better communicators than Democratic presidents.

_____

_____

_____

j. Too many people have been unable to find work.

_____

_____

_____

Exercise 2-4. Below you will find several paragraphs that might appear in a letter to the editor. Read the paragraphs, then answer the questions below.

The opioid crisis in the United States is getting worse with each passing year. Hundreds of millions of opioid prescriptions have been written by doctors each year, and those prescriptions lead to overdoses. Over the last twenty years, more Americans have been overdosing on opioid prescriptions. The availability of heroin and synthetic opioids like fentanyl make the problem even worse. We should be devoting more resources to crisis response, with a special emphasis on rehabilitation. When lives are at stake, especially our young people, the government must act.

Anyone who pays any attention to national news has seen countless stories of lives destroyed by opioid addiction. The federal government should provide more resources to state and local health care agencies that have been overwhelmed in the crisis. The most important factor in solving the crisis is rehabilitation for those suffering through opioid addiction. Only by offering the necessary support to help those in need will we be able to reverse the trend of increasing overdose deaths.

The opioid crisis is the most important domestic policy issue facing our country and must be addressed before more lives are lost.

a. Identify two normative statements or claims from the preceding text that cannot be tested empirically as currently expressed.

_____

_____

_____

_____

_____

b. Write down two statements or claims in the preceding text that are empirical and can be tested.

_____

_____

_____

_____

_____

Exercise 2-5. Many people make the following claim: "You cannot predict human behavior." In light of our discussion of the scientific approach to political science, do you find this claim to be valid? (*Hint:* Try breaking human behavior down into more specific traits or properties. For example, consider if people are naturally aggressive. Then think of ways that this might be empirically investigated.)

_____

_____

_____

_____

_____

_____

_____

_____

Exercise 2-6.   Chapter 2 of the textbook highlights criticisms of the empirical study of political science.

a.   List the criticisms of the empirical study of political science here.

_____

_____

_____

_____

_____

b.   Which of the criticisms do you find most compelling and why?

_____

_____

_____

_____

_____

HELPFUL HINTS
DECODING THE AMBIGUITY OF POLITICAL DISCOURSE

As we stated earlier, political discourse is frequently ambiguous, and you have to think carefully about what words really say. Sometimes a politician's meaning is clear. Consider President Obama's Rose Garden speech on a proposed nuclear deal with Iran.[1] In his speech President Obama said, "The Islamic Republic of Iran has been advancing its nuclear program for decades," which was a straightforward factual statement that could be verified empirically. But he also claimed, "I made clear that we were prepared to resolve this issue diplomatically, but only if Iran came to the table in a serious way." The word _serious_ makes this statement a judgment, not a factual proposition. Whether something is serious or not is an opinion. In some people's minds, Iran had been making serious attempts at diplomacy, but others thought differently. Who was right? It is hard to see how the proposition could be scientifically proven true or false.

Exercise 2-7.   Chapter 2 in the textbook focuses on empirical research and using the scientific method. Empiricism is defined as "relying on observation to verify propositions." In this exercise you will want to consider *how* you might make observations to verify propositions. For each of the following empirical statements, indicate where you might look or how you might make observations to find information to verify the statement. In the example below, you will see that while you only need to provide one answer, there are many potential verification methods.

Example: A majority of voters oppose the use of the death penalty.

Answer: "I would search for survey results on national news organization Web sites," or "I would randomly sample students at my university and ask if they support the death penalty," or "I would call an interest group that focuses on the death penalty and ask about support for the death penalty among voters."

a.   More voters are registered with the Democratic Party than the Republican Party in Pennsylvania.

_____

_____

b.   The British Parliament currently has more than twelve parties represented by members.

_____

_____

c.   Someone working forty hours a week and earning the minimum wage will still be below the federal poverty level for a family of two.

_____

_____

d.   People are not willing to pay higher taxes to address climate change.

_____

_____

e.   Texas has the most stringent voter identification law in the United States.

_____

_____

f.   Ninety percent of deaths attributed to diarrheal diseases like cholera are children five years of age or younger.

_____

_____

Exercise 2-8.   In order to think about the scientific components of empirical research it is useful to compare research projects that are more scientific with projects that are less scientific. For this exercise you will compare *two* examples of empirical research with publicly available results on the Internet.

The first survey is part of Gallup's research on worldwide migration using the Gallup World Poll. You can download a pdf copy of the report, called *Gallup Migration Report*, from the student Web site at https://edge.sagepub.com/johnson9e. You will also find a second pdf file, *Gallup World Poll*, that describes the methodology behind the survey results.

The second survey is an online instant poll created by HGTV Magazine that asked respondents to choose their favorite chair. Web site readers were asked to choose their favorite among four options—wingback, slipper, barrel, and Chinese Chippendale—and then the results were made available to the reader. The results were wingback (59.2%); slipper (18.4%); barrel (16.5%); and Chinese Chippendale (4.7%). No additional information about the poll was available on the Web site.

Compare and contrast the scientific nature of each project. Make sure to describe the scientific components each project made use of, such as random samples, replicability, generalization, etc.

_____

_____

_____

_____

_____

_____

_____

_____

NOTE

1.   The White House, "Statement by the President on the Framework to Prevent Iran from Obtaining a Nuclear Weapon," April 2, 2015, www.whitehouse.gov/the-press-office/2015/04/02/statement-president-framework-prevent-iran-obtaining-nuclear-weapon.

3 BEGINNING THE RESEARCH PROCESS

Identifying a Research Topic, Developing Research Questions, and Reviewing the Literature

Many would agree that picking and narrowing a topic are two of the hardest tasks confronting a new researcher. One can, of course, easily identify issues worthy of research, such as the war on terror or the effects of television on democracy. But moving from a desire to "do something on _____" to a specific theme that can be researched with relatively few resources and little time can be quite challenging.

Part of the difficulty lies in having enough information about the subject matter. What is already known about it? How have previous investigators studied it? What important questions remain unanswered? All these considerations motivate the review of the literature.

Chapter 3 of the textbook provides readers with some insights and tips for conducting an effective literature review. It is particularly important that you understand the differences between different kinds of sources, such as scholarly and mass circulation publications.

As mentioned in the textbook chapter, you can easily enough use Google or an equivalent search engine to search for *terrorism* or *television* or any other subject. But these efforts are usually unsuccessful because they lead to too much irrelevant information. Instead, we encourage the application of more specialized databases and library tools.

Exercise 3-1.   For this exercise you will begin thinking about how to find a research question for a research paper. One potential source for ideas is a political news Web site. Visit an online political news organization like Politico.com or BBC.com. On the lines following, write six research questions based on political news stories from the organization you selected. The research questions should be political in nature.

1. Article title:

   _____

   _____

   Research question:

   _____

   _____

2. Article title:

   _____

   _____

   Research question:

   _____

   _____

3. Article title:

   _____

   _____

Research question:

_____

_____

4. Article title:

_____

_____

Research question:

_____

_____

5. Article title:

_____

_____

Research question:

_____

_____

6. Article title:

_____

_____

Research question:

_____

_____

HELPFUL HINTS
THE BALANCE BETWEEN FINDING TOO FEW AND TOO MANY SOURCES

Students often wonder, "How many sources do I need in a literature review?" While we cannot give you a precise number, we can help you think about how to direct your search for sources. There is a balance to be found between finding too few and too many sources. For example, suppose you follow our advice in chapter 3 of the textbook and the boxed feature titled "Pyramid Citations." Remember that by *pyramid* we mean that each time you find what appears to be a useful source, you look at its list of notes and references, which, in turn, may point to two or more additional sources, and so on. Even if you start with a small list, you can quickly assemble a huge list of sources. You may soon find yourself overwhelmed with potential sources. How can you rapidly work through the sources? One way is to rely on the abstract. If a journal includes abstracts for articles, you can swiftly scan an abstract and determine if the source will be useful to you.

Exercise 3-2.   A potential source for research topic ideas is a political science journal. For this exercise we will examine articles published in *Comparative Political Studies*. First, find each cited article and read its abstract. Second, identify the research question and think about related questions that are unanswered in each project. Finally, write down three potential research questions that are related to each of the two articles.

First article:
Celeste L. Arrington, "Hiding in Plain Sight: Pseudonymity and Participation in Legal Mobilization," *Comparative Political Studies* 52, no. 2 (February 2019): 310–41. doi:10.1177/0010414018774356

a. Identify the research question in this article:

_____

_____

b. Next, think about how you might investigate a similar topic. Write down three new research questions below.

1. _____

2. _____

3. _____

Second article:
Gizem Arikan, and Pazit Ben-Nun Bloom, "Religion and Political Protest: A Cross-Country Analysis," *Comparative Political Studies* 52, no. 2 (February 2019): 246–76. doi:10.1177/0010414018774351

c. Identify the research question in this article:

_____

_____

d. Next, think about how you might investigate a similar topic. Write down three new research questions below.

1. _____

2. _____

3. _____

Exercise 3-3.   Literature reviews are an important part of the research process. They provide the context and background so that a research project furthers our understanding of a political phenomenon by, among other things, attempting to resolve conflicting evidence, investigating a topic in different settings and populations, or using different measures of key concepts.

The first step is to find a copy of Andrew Menger, Robert M. Stein, and Greg Vonnahme's "Reducing the Undervote with Vote by Mail," *American Politics Research* 46, no. 6 (November 2018): 1,039–64. Next, read the literature review section, "Theories Explaining Undervoting" and "The Effect of Mail Balloting on Undervoting," on pages 1,041 through 1,043. After reading the literature review section, answer the following questions.

a. How have previous analyses explained the causes of undervoting? What is the consensus in the literature?

_____

_____

_____

b. The authors wrote, "Researchers have found many of these explanations are mitigated by social and demographic traits of voters and their affective predispositions." Why is it important that the authors identified mitigating factors?

_____

_____

_____

c. How many studies have previously analyzed ballot completion under all-mail elections? Did these studies have similar findings? If not, how were the findings different?

_____

_____

_____

Exercise 3-4.   Suppose you are working as a research assistant for a political science professor who is beginning a new book about the current state of income inequality in the United States. She needs to make sure that she has read as much serious analytic writing as possible and wants you to begin compiling a bibliography of published materials. Which of the following potential sources would you add to the list? Why? For each source below, indicate if it should be on the high priority list (a list of the most important analytic treatments) or on the low priority list (a list of less important sources). Explain your reasoning.

a. Economist Thomas Piketty's 2014 book _Capital in the Twenty-First Century_

_____

_____

b. A 2013 National Public Radio interview transcript with economist Tyler Cowan, author of _Average Is Over_

_____

_____

c. Thomas Edsall's review in the _New York Times_ of Joseph Stiglitz's 2012 book, _The Price of Inequality_

_____

_____

d. A report titled *The Truth about Income Inequality*, produced by the Center of the American Experiment

_____

_____

e. A 2015 article titled "The Fiscal Disadvantage of Young Italians: A New View on Consolidation and Fairness," published in the *Journal of Economic Inequality*

_____

_____

f. Jill Lepore's article "Richer and Poorer, Accounting for Inequality," in *New Yorker* magazine

_____

_____

g. A news article by Jim Siegel in the *Columbus Dispatch* about income inequality in Ohio titled "Income Gap Less in Ohio but Growing Everywhere"

_____

_____

h. A 2014 editorial in the *Washington Times* titled "Obama's 'Income Inequality' Deeper from Bailing Out His Rich Wall Street Donors"

_____

_____

HELPFUL HINTS
FINDING SCHOLARLY SOURCES

The first step in finding scholarly sources is usually using a search engine or database specifically dedicated to scholarly work. These specialized tools include resources that are publicly available, such as Google Scholar, and tools that are available on a subscription basis, such as JSTOR. The best place for you to start depends on the resources available to you. Anyone can of course use publicly available tools like Google Scholar, but you might find it useful to check out the resources available at your school's library. Most colleges and universities maintain subscriptions to research tools for student use. Check with your library to see what is available to you—you will likely find that the minimal time spent learning about these resources will dramatically improve your research abilities.

Exercise 3-5. In this exercise you will examine a research article with respect to its citations to learn how to find related work. Literature reviews can be completed much more quickly if you can efficiently find research related to your topic of study. Imagine that you are interested in researching how people connect through social associations. You begin by finding one article written by Kwak, Shah, and Holbert that is directly related to your topic of interest. We will see how you can use one article as a starting point to find many more sources for your project. You should find the article using this citation: Nojin Kwak, Dhavan V. Shah, and R. Lance Holbert, "Connecting, Trusting, and Participating: The Direct and Interactive Effects of Social Associations," *Political Research Quarterly* 57, no. 4 (2004): 643–52.

The first step is to visit Google Scholar at https://scholar.google.com. Make sure the "Articles" radio button is selected rather than the "Case Law" radio button, then type the article title into the search bar and press enter. Once you have found the article, you are ready to answer the questions below. As you are answering the questions, think about how each answer could help you find additional materials for your own project.

a. Click on the article title to see the article abstract and citations. What kind of sources did Kwak, Shah, and Holbert cite, and in what fields of study were the citations located? In the space below, describe the kind of sources you found and list at least four academic fields of study you found among the citations.

_____

_____

_____

_____

_____

_____

b. Next, go back to the initial Google Scholar search result. Click on each author's name. You will find that each author has written many articles. When considering the other articles Kwak, Shah, and Holbert have each written, do the topics of those other articles seem related to "Connecting, Trusting, and Participating: The Direct and Interactive Effects of Social Associations?" What evidence did you use to make this judgment?

_____

_____

_____

_____

_____

_____

c. Finally, go back to the initial Google Scholar search result. Click on the "Cited By" and "Related Articles" links. Do the topics of the articles you found when clicking on the links seem related to "Connecting, Trusting, and Participating: The Direct and Interactive Effects of Social Associations?" What evidence did you use to make this judgment?

_____

_____

_____

_____

_____

_____

Exercise 3-6. Use Google Scholar to search for articles related to the role of civic culture in democracy. List five sources below using the *Chicago* citation style format. The first step is to search for sources using Google Scholar. Visit Google Scholar at https://scholar .google.com. Make sure the "Articles" radio button is selected rather than the "Case Law" radio button, then type "civic culture in democracy" into the search bar and press enter. Scan the results and pick five sources you think would be useful in the project. Once you have found five sources, you are ready to list the sources below. For each source, click on the quotation mark link. Clicking on this link will reveal the "Cite" box, in which you will find five different citation formats for the source, including the *Chicago* style. Use the *Chicago* style to record your five sources below.

1. _____

_____

2. _____

_____

3. _____

_____

4. _____

_____

5. _____

_____

Exercise 3-7. Suppose you are interning with your state's Office of the Attorney General. Your boss is interested in reviewing scientific evidence about the potential negative effects of voter identification laws because your state legislature is considering making the state's voter identification laws more stringent. Your task is to find relevant political science sources that can help inform your boss on the topic. Use Google Scholar to find five articles published in political science journals.

The first step is to visit Google Scholar at https://scholar.google.com. Make sure the "Articles" radio button is selected rather than the "Case Law" radio button, then type "voter identification" into the search bar and press enter. Scan the results and pick five sources you think would be useful in the project. Once you have found five sources, you are ready to list the sources below. For each source, click on the quotation mark link. Clicking on this link will reveal the "Cite" box, in which you will find five different citation formats for the source including the MLA style. Use the MLA style to record your five sources below.

1. _____

_____

2. _____

_____

3. _____

_____

4. _____

_____

5. _____

_____

Exercise 3-8. Imagine that you are enrolled in a political science class for which you choose to write a research paper on political violence. You have completed the initial stage of a literature review by collecting eight scholarly articles that address the causes of political violence. The next step is to start organizing your eight articles for your literature review. The table below includes notes on each of your eight sources. Notice that each cell includes important information about one article. Each cell includes the parenthetical citation in bold to identify the article, along with notes about the article's title, the research question, the time period studied, the unit of analysis and sample size of the study, the region of interest, whether the study took a quantitative or qualitative approach, the research design, and the article's conclusion. These notes serve as an example of the kinds of notes you should take on sources for a literature review and will help you answer the questions below. After you have answered the questions below, consider how you could combine the sentences you wrote into a literature review.

As we discussed in the textbook, a literature review should be organized around important topics rather than summarizing one individual article after another. Below you will find several topics you might include in a literature review—research question, time period, region under study, quantitative or qualitative approach, research design, points of agreement, and points of disagreement. For each topic, write a sentence or two that incorporate the sources in table 3-1 in the style of a literature review. Use the answer provided for question e as an example of the expected format. Make sure to include parenthetical citations like in question e.

TABLE 3-1 ■ Notes on Eight Scholarly Articles for Use in a Literature Review

Eck (2014)	**Ide (2015)**
Title: The Law of the Land: Communal Conflict and Legal Authority[1]	Title and research question: Why Do Conflicts over Scarce Renewable Resources Turn Violent?[2]
Research question: What are the causes of communal land conflict?	Time period (countries): 1990–2010 (20)
Time period (countries): 1990–2009 (16)	Region: Asia, Africa, Latin America, Middle East, and the Pacific
Region: West Africa	Quantitative or qualitative: Qualitative
Quantitative or qualitative: Quantitative	Research design: Fuzzy-set qualitative comparative analysis
Research design: Cross-sectional	Conclusion: The presence of two structural conditions (stable, collective identities for the use of violence by conflict parties and if one party had a low, hard, and relational power advantage) and one triggering condition (recent political change) is sufficient for the violent escalation of renewable resource conflicts. High power differences and external resource appropriation were not identified as robust conditions.
Conclusion: Competing jurisdictions with overlapping mandates 200–350% more likely to experience communal violence than single jurisdictions. Competing legal authority structures can enable violence and limit the ability of security forces to respond.	
Fox (2004)	**Muller (1985)**
Title: The Rise of Religious Nationalism and Conflict: Ethnic Conflict and Revolutionary Wars, 1945–2001[3]	Title: Income Inequality, Regime Repressiveness, and Political Violence[4]
Research question: What are the causes of communal land conflict?	Research question: How do income inequality and political repressiveness affect political violence?
Time period (ethnic minority groups): 1945–2001 (337)	Time period (countries): 1958–1962 (29) and 1968–1977 (51)
Region: World	Regions: Europe, North America, Latin America, Asia.
Quantitative or qualitative: Quantitative	Quantitative or qualitative: Quantitative
Research design: Cross-sectional	Research design: Cross-sectional
Conclusion: Religion can cause conflict, and its importance has increased over time: "Religious conflicts were less violent than other conflicts until around 1965, when they became more violent" (p. 727).	Conclusion: Income inequality and a regime structure that is somewhat but not totally repressive cause more political violence.

(Continued)

TABLE 3-1 ■ (Continued)

Fearon and Laitin (2003)	**Pearce (2005)**
Title: Ethnicity, Insurgency, and Civil War[5]	Title: Religious Rage: A Quantitative Analysis of the Intensity of Religious Conflicts[6]
Research question: What explains the recent prevalence of violent civil conflict around the world?	Research question: Does religion increase the intensity of political violence?
Time period (wars): 1945–1999 (127)	Time period (interstate and intrastate conflicts): 1946–2001 (278)
Region: World	Region: World
Quantitative or qualitative: Quantitative	Quantitative or qualitative: Quantitative
Research design: Cross-sectional	Research design: Cross-sectional time series
Conclusion: Conditions that favor insurgency include poverty, political instability, rough terrain, and large populations. Civil war is not caused by the end of the Cold War, ethnic or religious diversity, or strong ethnic or political grievances.	Conclusion: Conflict involving religion is more intense than other kinds of conflict. This relationship is not statistically significant when controlling for the relevance of religion in the conflict.
Homer-Dixon (1994)	**Welsh (2016)**
Title: Environmental Scarcities and Violent Conflict: Evidence from Cases[7]	Title: Local and National: Keroyokan Mobbing in Indonesia[8]
Research question: Could "environmental scarcities" precipitate violent civil or international conflict?	Research question: What are the causes of *keroyokan*—mobbing—a form of political violence?
Time period (ethnic minority groups): 1945–2001 (337)	Time period (countries): 1995–2004 (Indonesia)
Region: World	Region: East Asia
Quantitative or qualitative: Qualitative	Quantitative or qualitative: Qualitative
Research design: Process tracing; case studies	Research design: Three case studies of provinces
Conclusion: "Environmental scarcity causes violent conflict. This conflict tends to be persistent, diffuse, and sub-national" (p. 39). The degradation and depletion of environmental resources is only one source of environmental scarcity; two other important sources are population growth and unequal resource distribution (p. 40).	Conclusion: Mobbing is caused by the tacit approval of local political leaders and links to historical practices of mob violence that are socialized as acceptable actions.

a. Research question (the questions that are asked and answered in the literature)

_____

_____

_____

_____

_____

_____

b. Time period (the periods scholars have studied)

_____

_____

_____

_____

_____

_____

c. Region under study (the regions scholars have studied)

_____

_____

_____

_____

_____

_____

d. Quantitative or qualitative approach (how scholars have made empirical observations)

_____

_____

_____

_____

_____

_____

e. Research design (the research designs used to study political violence)

Scholars have used different research designs to observe and analyze national and subnational variation in the causes of political violence. While many have used cross-sectional analyses (Eck 2014; Fox 2004; Muller 1985; Fearon and Laitin 2003), cross-sectional time series analyses (Pearce 2005), or fuzzy-set qualitative comparative analysis (Ida 2015) to understand national variation in the causes of political violence, other scholars have used case studies (Homer-Dixon 1994; Welsh 2016) to analyze subnational variation.

f. Points of agreement (conclusions shared by more than one scholar)

_____

_____

_____

_____

_____

_____

g. Points of disagreement (conclusions that run counter to another conclusion)

_____

_____

_____

_____

_____

_____

NOTES

1. Kristine Eck, "The Law of the Land: Communal Conflict and Legal Authority," *Journal of Peace Research* 51, no. 4 (2014): 441–54. http://www.jstor.org/stable/24557472.

2. Tobias Ide, "Why Do Conflicts over Scarce Renewable Resources Turn Violent? A Qualitative Comparative Analysis," *Global Environmental Change* 33 (2015): 61–70.

3. Jonathan Fox, "The Rise of Religious Nationalism and Conflict: Ethnic Conflict and Revolutionary Wars, 1945–2001," *Journal of Peace Research* 41, no. 6 (November 2004): 715–31. doi:10.1177/0022343304047434

4. Edward N. Muller, "Income Inequality, Regime Repressiveness, and Political Violence," *American Sociological Review* 50, no. 1 (1985): 47–61. http://www.jstor.org/stable/2095339.

5. James D. Fearon and David D. Laitin, "Ethnicity, Insurgency, and Civil War," *American Political Science Review* 97, no. 1 (2003): 75–90. doi:10.1017/S0003055403000534

6. Susanna Pearce, "Religious Rage: A Quantitative Analysis of the Intensity of Religious Conflicts," *Terrorism and Political Violence* 17, no. 3 (2005): 333–52. doi:10.1080/09546550590929237

7. Thomas F. Homer-Dixon, "Environmental Scarcities and Violent Conflict: Evidence from Cases," *International Security* 19, no. 1 (1994): 5–40. doi:10.2307/2539147

8. Bridget Welsh, "Local and National: Keroyokan Mobbing in Indonesia," *Journal of East Asian Studies* 8, no. 3 (2008): 473–504. doi:10.1017/S1598240800006512

THE BUILDING BLOCKS OF SOCIAL SCIENTIFIC RESEARCH

Hypotheses, Concepts, Variables, and Measurements

In chapter 4 of the textbook, we explored some initial steps in the research process: how one may start with an interest in a political phenomenon or political concept, pose a research question, propose an answer to the question in the form of a hypothesis, and devise a measurement strategy using variables. A variable is a concept whose value is not constant; rather, it varies. Informed or suggested by theory or casual observation, hypotheses are guesses about relationships between variables. Hypotheses should be written so that the nature of the proposed relationship is clear, the concepts are distinct, and the unit of analysis is identified. Concepts or variables are attributes of an entity—something or someone—that is called a *unit of analysis*. For example, units of analysis can be countries, cities, individuals, members of legislatures or courts, speeches, or government actions and activities.

Measurement involves deciding how to measure the presence, absence, or number of concepts in a research project. Two important concerns with measures are reliability and validity. A reliable measure yields a consistent, stable result as long as the concept being measured remains unchanged. Measurement strategies that rely on memories, for example, may be quite unreliable because the ability to remember specific information may vary depending on when the measurement is made and whether distractions are present. Valid measures correspond well with the meaning of the concept being measured. Researchers often develop rather elaborate schemes to measure complex concepts.

Level of measurement is also an important aspect of a measurement scheme. There are four levels of measurement. From lowest to highest, these levels are as follows: nominal, ordinal, interval, and ratio. Choosing the appropriate statistics for the analysis of data depends on knowing the level of measurement of your variables. Frequently a variable can be measured using a variety of schemes. Choosing the scheme that uses the highest level of measurement possible provides the most information and is the most precise measure of a concept. Researchers frequently recode data, thus changing the level of measurement of a variable.

Exercise 4-1.   Chapter 4 includes many technical terms that may at first glance be somewhat confusing. Students are often confused about the differences between some of the more similar-sounding terms. Below you will find pairs of similar-sounding terms. Provide an explanation for how these terms are different.

a.   Antecedent variable and intervening variable

_____

_____

b.   Independent variable and dependent variable

_____

_____

c.   Hypothesis and directional hypothesis

_____

_____

d.   Validity and reliability

_____

_____

Exercise 4-2.   Chapter 4 focuses on the construction of hypotheses. In this exercise you will assess the research question below and generate hypotheses you would want to test.

a.   In the space provided, write six hypotheses you would want to test to answer the question provided. In writing your hypotheses, pay close attention to the six characteristics of a good hypothesis as discussed in the textbook: (1) empirical, (2) general, (3) plausible, (4) specific, (5) stated as intended for testing, and (6) testable. Also, try to generate hypotheses that include different dependent variables related to the research question. For example, consider different kinds of political participation that may have different motivating factors (independent variables).

Research question: Why do citizens participate in politics?

1.   _____

_____

2.   _____

_____

3.   _____

_____

4.   _____

_____

5.   _____

_____

6.   _____

_____

b.   Specify the unit of analysis for your research question and hypotheses. (*Hint:* The unit of analysis should be consistent across the question, theory, and hypotheses.)

_____

_____

HELPFUL HINTS
IDENTIFYING VARIABLES AND UNITS OF ANALYSIS

An empirical hypothesis has three distinct components: the unit of analysis, the independent variable, and the dependent variable. First, remember that the population of interest in a hypothesis is the unit of analysis for the research project. Second, remember that independent variables are the measurements of the phenomena that are thought to *influence, affect,* or *cause* some other phenomenon. A dependent variable is thought *to be caused, to depend upon,* or *to be a function of* an independent variable. Finally, something cannot be both a unit of analysis and a variable. Something cannot be both an independent and a dependent variable.

Exercise 4-3.   In this exercise you will consider the difference between variables and a unit of analysis. You will find below a series of hypotheses. For each hypothesis identify the independent variable, the dependent variable, and the unit of analysis. When doing so, keep in mind the following:

Example: An increase in a person's education causes an increase in a person's income.

Answer: Independent variable: education; dependent variable: income; unit of analysis: individuals

a.   Laws that limit individual behavior are more likely to be overturned in court than other laws.

b.   Countries with more square miles of forest spend more money on fire prevention than other countries.

c.   Senior citizens are more likely to read news stories about Social Security than younger citizens.

d.   Cities with more bridges are more likely to face budget deficits related to infrastructure spending.

e.   Legislation sponsored by recently elected members of a legislature is less likely to pass on the floor of the legislature.

f.   Interest groups that collect membership dues are more likely to participate in direct lobbying activities.

Exercise 4-4.   Each of the following hypotheses is faulty in some way. Some do not specify the relationship between the variables (correlation or causation), some do not specify the direction of the relationship (positive or negative), and some are too specific, tautological, or normative, or simply do not make sense. Explain which fault is found in each hypothesis.

a.   There is a positive relationship between agricultural subsidies and authoritarianism.

b.   The governor of my state is responsible for raising my taxes.

c.   Violent crime has increased in Spain because there are more violent crimes.

d. States with more breweries are more likely to elect judges rather than use an appointment system.

_____

_____

e. There is a causal relationship between health care deductibles and number of doctor visits.

_____

_____

f. Countries with more free trade agreements are better than those with fewer agreements.

_____

_____

Exercise 4-5.   For each pair of variables, write a hypothesis that defines the relationship between the variables (correlation or causation) and the direction of the relationship.

a. Number of violent crimes in a community; support for the death penalty

_____

b. Number of people addicted to opioids; money spent on drug treatment programs

_____

c. Likelihood of a veto; legislation that limits civil liberties

_____

d. Number of National Labor Relations Board (NLRB) members appointed by a Republican president; likelihood of pro-labor decision by the NLRB

_____

e. Income level; financial contribution to a congressional candidate

_____

Exercise 4-6.   Below are sets of three variables. On the lines after each set, do the following:

- Write a hypothesis relating the first two variables.
- Identify independent and dependent variables.
- State how you expect the third variable to affect the hypothesized relationship.

- Draw an arrow diagram that includes all three variables.

- Determine whether the third variable is antecedent, intervening, or alternative.

a. Primary caregiver for children (primary caregiver, not primary caregiver); support for Family Medical Leave Law (thermometer scale for support); gender (female, male)

_____

_____

_____

b. Intention to vote in upcoming election; respondent's general interest in politics; predicted outcome of election ("too close to call," "somewhat competitive," "lopsided victory")

_____

_____

_____

c. Type of lightbulb purchased (regular, energy efficient); difference in cost of regular and high-efficiency lightbulbs (small difference, large difference); concern about global climate change

_____

_____

_____

Exercise 4-7.   Write a research question that uses each of the following units of analysis:

a. Individuals

_____

b. Countries

_____

c. Treaties

_____

d. Organizations

_____

Exercise 4-8.   What is the level of measurement of the following measures? If you think there could be more than one level of measurement, explain your answer.

a.   Religion (Christian, Hindu, Jewish, Muslim, other)

_____

_____

b.   Number of nongovernmental organizations operating in a country (0–10, 11–20, 21–30, 31 or more)

_____

_____

c.   Intelligence measured as IQ (0–200)

_____

_____

d.   Money raised by a political action committee during an election cycle (dollars)

_____

_____

e.   Number of ministers in a cabinet

_____

_____

f.   Number of natural disasters in a country during a calendar year (0–10, 11–20, 21–30, more than 30)

_____

_____

g.   Party identification (Conservative, Labour, other)

_____

_____

h.   Number of border crossings along a border

_____

_____

i. Political ideology (very liberal, liberal, moderate, conservative, very conservative)

_____

_____

j. Percentage of citizens currently incarcerated

_____

_____

k. Year country joined the African Union

_____

_____

l. Number of governments in a country since 1800

_____

_____

m. Primary policy objective of military intervention (foreign policy restraint, humanitarian intervention, internal political change)

_____

_____

n. Type of income tax system (flat tax, progressive, other)

_____

_____

o. Year in college (freshman, sophomore, junior, senior)

_____

_____

p. Health care system (government-managed health care, health care coverage required by law, private health care system)

_____

_____

Exercise 4-9. Levels of measurement are important because they serve as a way to think about both the amount of information available in a measure and the mathematical properties of the measure. In this exercise you are going to consider the amount of information available in two different variables that measure education with different levels of measurement.

Consider these two variables that both measure education:

Variable #1: What is your highest completed level of education? (Respondent picks one of the six levels of education.)

1. No formal education

2. Elementary school

3. Middle school

4. High school

5. College

6. Advanced degree

Variable #2: How many years of formal education have you completed? (Respondent supplies the number of years of education.)

For each of the variables above, first identify the level of measurement. Second, one of the two variables provides more information to the analyst than the other about the level of education each respondent has accomplished. Identify the variable that captures more information about education and explain why.

a. Variable #1 level of measurement: _____

b. Variable #2 level of measurement: _____

c. Which variable captures more information about education, Variable #1 or Variable #2? Explain your answer.

_____

_____

_____

_____

Exercise 4-10.   *Conceptualization* is the process of defining a term, and *operationalization* is determining the rules by which a concept is measured and scores assigned. Generally, a researcher first defines a term then decides how to measure the term once the definition is in hand. Some concepts are quite easy to define and measure because they have widely accepted definitions and are concrete terms. For example, consider the concept of age:

Conceptualization: Age is the number of years someone has been alive.

Operationalization: I will measure age by asking a question—"How old are you in years?"—then I will record the number of years the respondent has been alive.

Other concepts are much more difficult because the definitions are not as widely accepted or the terms are more abstract. Let us consider how to conceptualize and operationalize the term *democracy*. To provide some context, imagine that we are interested in variation in democracy across countries. In the appropriate space below, conceptualize and operationalize *democracy*. Remember that the operationalization should include all parts of the definition.

Conceptualize *democracy*:

_____

_____

Operationalize *democracy*:

_____

_____

_____

_____

Exercise 4-11. Suppose you think that moral values are theoretically important in explaining voting behavior. Before you can write your theory or test your hypothesis involving moral values, you must conceptualize and operationalize the concept. In the space following, conceptualize (define the term) and operationalize (decide how you will record the quantitative variable) moral values.

a. Conceptualize *moral values*:

_____

_____

_____

b. Operationalize *moral values*:

_____

_____

_____

_____

Exercise 4-12. Operationalization is deciding how to record empirical observations of the occurrence of an attribute or a behavior using numerals or scores. In other words, it is deciding how to move from defined concept to quantifiable variable. In this exercise you are going to consider the challenges involved in quantifying both concrete and abstract concepts that are commonly used in political science research. You will find below a series of conceptualized terms. Your job is to explain how you would operationalize each term for use in a survey research project by creating the questions that would yield the appropriate variable for each concept. (*Hint:* Concrete terms are much easier to work with than abstract terms. Pay close attention to the abstract terms, such as *ideology* and *efficacy*.)

Example: Voter registration: Whether someone is currently registered to vote.

Answer: Ask each respondent to indicate whether he or she is currently registered to vote by asking, "Are you currently registered to vote in your state?" (1) "Yes, I am registered to vote," (0) "No, I am not registered to vote."

a. Female: Female or not

_____

_____

_____

b. Household income: The amount of money earned by all members of a household in a year

_____

_____

_____

c. Race: The race each respondent most closely identifies with

_____

_____

_____

d. Ideology: A set of beliefs and ideas, including one's moral code and worldview. The most important issues and ideas involve how the government should address those unable to provide food, health care, and housing for themselves and their children. The extent to which the government should extend services to support those in need in these areas makes up the worldview.

_____

_____

_____

e. Political efficacy: The belief that one's political action will have a meaningful effect. In particular, I define political action as interpersonal communication with elected officials.

_____

_____

_____

HELPFUL HINTS
RECODING DATA

There are two strategies for recoding data to combine or collapse categories of a measure:

1. **Theoretical**. Choose categories that are meaningfully distinct, where theory would tell you that the differences between the categories are important or where you can see that there are distinct clusters of scores or values. For example, when combining actual household income amounts into income levels, a researcher might consider what the official poverty level is and group all households with incomes below that level into the lowest income group.

2. **Equally sized categories**. Choose categories so that each category has roughly an equal number of cases. In addition, limit the number of categories so that each category has at least ten cases.

Exercise 4-13.   Table 4-1 contains environmental scores for South American countries from the 2018 Environmental Performance Index (EPI). The EPI scores are based upon performance indicators for environmental health and ecosystem vitality. The scores are calculated using data about each country gathered from international organizations, research institutions, academia, and government agencies. While the calculation of the score is somewhat complex, we need only know that the index is an interval-level variable and higher scores mean better environmental protection.

Suppose you wanted to recode this interval-level variable into an *ordinal-level variable* with *at least three categories*. When one recodes data, one begins with a coded variable, such as the interval-level EPI score, and converts the values for each case into a different variable. In this case, you would convert the values into an ordinal-level variable. How could you do this? In the space below, you will explain how you decided to create an ordinal-level variable (the logic of how you created the categories for the ordinal variable) and recode the data by ordinal-level scores in the last column for each case on the data table. Remember that ordinal-level variables have categories. Create at least three labeled categories.

a. How would you recode the interval-level variable into an ordinal-level variable with at least three categories? (*Hint:* Do not forget to label each category!)

_____

_____

_____

_____

_____

b. Recode the EPI score variable in table 4-1 into an ordinal-level measure.

TABLE 4-1 ■ Environmental Performance Index (EPI) Scores in South American Countries, 2018		
Country	**EPI Score Interval**	**EPI Score Ordinal**
Colombia	65.22	
Uruguay	64.65	
Venezuela	63.89	
Peru	61.92	
Brazil	60.70	
Argentina	59.30	
Chile	57.49	
Ecuador	57.42	
Bolivia	55.98	
Suriname	54.20	
Guyana	47.93	

Source: EPI data available at https://epi.envirocenter.yale.edu/epi-topline.

Exercise 4-14.   Table 4-2 shows the distribution of the top twenty countries by GDP in 2017 in constant 2010 U.S. dollars according to World Bank data. In this exercise you will consider how data can be recoded for analysis. The two data columns on the left of the table include country name and GDP in millions, which is a ratio-level variable. Your job is to think about how you could recode the ratio-level measure of GDP into two different ordinal-level variables—one with four categories and one with three categories. The goal is to see that you can manipulate ratio-level data to help think about the data in different ways. In the space below, explain how you created your two ordinal-level measures. Remember that ordinal-level variables have ordered categories. What categories did you use for each variable, and what values did you assign to each category? (*Hint:* Do not forget to label each category!)

a.   GDP ordinal 1 explanation (four categories): _____

_____

_____

_____

b.   GDP ordinal 2 explanation (three categories): _____

_____

_____

_____

c.   Recode the GDP data below in the appropriate column based on your explanations in parts a and b.

TABLE 4-2 ■ Top Twenty Countries by GDP (Constant 2010 U.S. Dollars) in 2017			
Country	**GDP (million)**	**GDP Ordinal 1**	**GDP Ordinal 2**
United States	17,304,984.28		
China	10,161,012.76		
Japan	6,156,328.72		
Germany	3,865,759.08		
France	2,857,089.40		
United Kingdom	2,806,903.10		
India	2,629,542.21		
Brazil	2,278,936.37		
Italy	2,111,901.94		
Canada	1,883,707.91		
Russian Federation	1,680,005.30		
Spain	1,509,201.53		
Australia	1,375,718.25		
Korea, Rep.	1,345,945.67		
Mexico	1,284,678.35		
Turkey	1,205,786.80		
Indonesia	1,090,459.49		
Netherlands	918,283.87		
Saudi Arabia	684,993.60		
Switzerland	649,067.88		

Source: World Bank, 2018, https://data.worldbank.org/indicator/NY.GDP.MKTP.KD?view=map&year_high_desc=true.

Exercise 4-15.   Below you will find a series of hypotheses. For each hypothesis identify the variables you would need to test the hypothesis and explain how you could measure each variable. When explaining your measurement strategy, be careful to consider validity and reliability.

a.   Small business owners are more likely to support tax cuts than other voters.

_____

_____

_____

_____

_____

b.   The availability of government-subsidized childcare causes household income to rise.

_____

_____

_____

_____

_____

c.   An increase in the number of nongovernmental organizations operating in an authoritarian state increases the rate at which the state democratizes.

_____

_____

_____

_____

_____

d.   Access to clean drinking water causes life expectancy to increase.

_____

_____

_____

_____

_____

_____

_____

5 SAMPLING

Verifying statements empirically lies at the core of modern political science. Abstract theorizing is a valuable, even necessary, activity. Still, most social scientists feel that at some point theories have to "face reality." Carefully observing and collecting data is an integral part of the research process.

Unfortunately, in all too many situations it is not possible to observe each member of a population. Hence, sampling—the process of drawing a small set of cases from a larger population—is necessary.

The social sciences depend heavily on sampling. This fact sometimes troubles the general public. "How," many citizens ask, "can you make a claim about all 322 million people in the United States when you've interviewed just five hundred of them?" Some people, however, including many reporters, politicians, and political advisers, act as though polling is an exact science. Chapter 5 of the textbook addresses these issues.

More specifically, sampling raises two questions. First, *how* should the subset of observations be collected from the population, and, second, *how reliable and valid* are inferences made on the basis of a sample? The first question pertains to sample types or designs, whereas the second deals with statistics and probability.

By working through these exercises, you should begin to get a feel for the basics of sampling techniques and their properties. These exercises do not require mathematical sophistication, but they do require careful thought.

Exercise 5-1. Sometimes students can be confused by terms that describe similar but distinctly different concepts. This confusion is often exacerbated when it comes to methodological terms. This exercise is about reinforcing your understanding of similar terms. For each of the word pairs below, define each term and then explain the important differences between them.

a. Population parameter and estimator

_____

_____

_____

b. Sampling frame and sampling unit

_____

_____

_____

c. Element and stratum

_____

_____

_____

d. Probability sample and nonprobability sample

_____

_____

_____

e. Proportionate and disproportionate sample

_____

_____

_____

Exercise 5-2.   Generally, political scientists prefer to use probability samples whenever possible to make causal inferences. In this exercise you will consider how you might make use of nonprobability sampling methods. The text describes four kinds of random sampling technique (simple random sample, systematic sample, stratified sample, cluster sample) and four nonprobability sampling techniques (purposive, convenience, quota, and snowball). Below you will find a description of eight samples. Label each example with the sampling technique listed above that best matches the example.

a. Selecting every twentieth person who exits a polling station to interview him or her about vote choices

_____

b. Hand-selecting participants in an experiment based on race, gender, and education level so that the sample mirrors the population on those three characteristics

_____

c. Asking a neighbor who homeschools her children about her opinion on state education policy, then asking for additional homeschoolers' contact information to find more participants for the study

_____

d. Randomly selecting Florida and Ohio from all fifty states; randomly selecting Miami-Dade County and Franklin County from a list of all counties in Florida and Ohio; and randomly selecting 750 respondents in Miami-Dade County, Florida, and randomly selecting 750 respondents in Franklin County, Ohio

_____

e. Drawing counties at random from a list of all counties in California to examine the effects of water policy on water usage

_____

f. A professor asking the 135 members of her class to complete a survey on political attitudes

_____

g. Randomly selecting 72 percent of a sample from a list of male legislators and 28 percent of a sample from a list of female legislators

_____

h. Choosing the Washington, Lincoln, F. D. Roosevelt, and Johnson presidencies as cases to study the president at war because they are the most interesting cases

_____

Exercise 5-3.   The following is an excerpt from an article by Laura Beth Nielsen titled "Situating Legal Consciousness: Experiences and Attitudes of Ordinary Citizens about Law and Street Harassment."[1] Read the excerpt and answer the questions that follow.

IV. METHOD

The empirical study of legal consciousness presents several methodological challenges. Legal consciousness is complex and difficult to inquire about without inventing it for the subjects, or, at the very least, biasing the subjects' responses. Only through in-depth interviews can legal consciousness emerge, leaving the researcher with lengthy transcripts and the daunting task of using them to determine how to gauge variation in legal consciousness and how this relates to broader social structures.

- Early studies attempted to capture the complexities of legal consciousness through observation and in-depth interviews with small samples (see Ewick and Silbey 1992; White 1991; Merry 1990; Sarat 1990). These methods were necessary as theories of legal consciousness were developing. More recently, scholars of legal consciousness have begun to advocate broader data collection to understand variation in legal consciousness and to map the relationship between consciousness and social structure (McCann 1999; Ewick & Silbey 1998; McCann & March 1996). In contrast, studies of political tolerance have surveyed large, randomly selected samples of citizens. The structured protocols of this line of research document attitudes and opinions, but do not allow for an in-depth understanding of legal consciousness.

- I bridge this gap by using qualitative research techniques to probe the complexity of legal consciousness, while also interviewing a large enough number of subjects of different races, genders, and classes (n = 100) to begin to gauge variation in it. The combination of field observation and in-depth interviews proved especially valuable. The field observations allowed me to witness and record various types of interactions between strangers in public places. Because I observed many subjects being harassed in public and their reactions to such comments, I was able to guard against the tendency some subjects might have had to inflate the bravado with which they responded to such comments. Of course, simply observing was not sufficient because I needed to learn how the subjects _experienced_ such interactions,

not simply how they responded. The in-depth interviews provided an opportunity to gain an understanding of how individuals think about such interactions, resulting in a "mutuality" between participant observation and in-depth interviews (Lofland & Lofland 1995).

- I systematically sampled subjects from the public places I observed. This strategy has several advantages. First, I knew that the subjects were consumers of public space, and thus they constituted a set of potential targets for offensive public speech. From my observations at different locations at different times, I also had some appreciation for what the subjects experienced. Second, by approaching subjects in person, I could establish rapport in a way that would have been impossible if I had initiated contact by telephone. This rapport was essential, given the sensitive nature of the interview questions. Asking subjects about experiences with offensive racist and sexist speech required speaking bluntly and using racial epithets as examples. It would have been difficult to gain consent without such personal contact.

- I followed systematic procedures to construct a sample that, while not a probability sample, included different types of people and minimized the possibility of researcher-biased selections because of my personal prepossessions and characteristics. Of course, my presence in the public spaces might have altered the nature of the interactions that took place. Yet in most instances I was simply another person in the crowd and did not have much impact on the obvious interactions taking place.

- I conducted a detailed assessment of data sites with the objective of maximizing variation in the socioeconomic status of potential subjects and guarding against idiosyncratic factors that might bias the results (Lofland & Lofland 1995). First, I selected field sites in a variety of locations in three communities in the San Francisco, California, Bay Area (Orinda, Berkeley/Oakland, and San Francisco) to insure broad representation across race, socioeconomic status, and gender among subjects selected to participate in the interviews. Second, I varied the day of the week, going to each of the locations on weekdays and weekends. Third, I varied the time of day by observing in each location during day, evening, and night hours. The field sites I selected were public places, such as sidewalks, public transportation terminals, and bus stops. Finally, to guard against approaching only potential subjects with whom I felt comfortable and to randomize subject selection within field sites, I devised a system whereby each person in the site had an equal chance of being approached.* I selected individuals to approach and asked whether they would participate in an interview about interactions among strangers in public places. I continued such selections until I achieved numerical goals for respondents with certain racial and gender characteristics. I oversampled white women and people of color for analytic purposes. Thus, even though I randomized selections within demographic subgroups and within strategically selected locations, this was not a random sample.**

_____

*When I entered a field site, I recorded the scene in my field notes, noting the date, time of day, location, and characteristics of the people occupying that location. I also noted all instances of street harassment. I observed interactions, noting the types of individuals who made comments to strangers, and what responses they received. To determine whom to approach, I randomly selected a side of the location (north or south, east or west) by the flip of a coin. I rolled a die to determine the interval among individuals I would approach; for example, if the coin came up "heads" I went to the north side of the location (such as a train platform); then, if the die came up "3," I approached every third person to ask if he or she would be willing to participate.

**In the analyses that follow, I emphasize comparisons across race and gender and limit the statistical analysis to simple chi-square tests for differences across groups. Given the size of the sample, the results should be seen as suggestive in a statistical sense and worthy of examination in larger sample designs.

a. What type of sample did the author use?

_____

_____

b. How did she try to limit bias in her sample?

_____

_____

_____

_____

_____

_____

_____

c. How did the author's method of selecting her subjects ensure that they were appropriate for her study?

_____

_____

_____

_____

_____

_____

_____

_____

Exercise 5-4.   Consider this hypothesis: _High school students have political beliefs and attitudes similar to those of their parents._ To test this hypothesis, both students and parents will be sent questionnaires and their responses compared. The work will be done at "South High," which has an enrollment of 2,000. Here are some ideas for collecting the data. In each instance identify the sampling design and indicate whether it would produce data for a satisfactory test of the hypothesis. Briefly explain your answer. To what populations, if any, could the results be generalized? (_Note:_ Do not worry about aspects of the project such as how questionnaires will be matched or obtaining permissions from the school board and/or others.)

a. Proposed sampling scheme: The investigator takes the first and last names (and addresses) from every other page of South High's student directory and mails a questionnaire to those students and their parents.

_____

_____

_____

_____

_____

_____

b. Proposed sampling scheme: Beginning March 1 at 3:30, the investigator stands outside the entrance to South High and hands out questionnaires to passing students and asks that they and their parents return them.

_____

_____

_____

_____

_____

_____

c. Proposed sampling scheme: Investigator asks South High's assistant principal to generate a random list of 200 student names and addresses. Each of these students and his or her parents are mailed a questionnaire.

_____

_____

_____

_____

_____

_____

d. Proposed sampling scheme: The investigator asks the guidance counselor for the names of exactly fifty college-prep students, fifty general study students, fifty vocational educational students, and fifty other students of any kind.

_____

_____

_____

_____

_____

e. Proposed sampling scheme: The investigator asks South High's assistant principal to draw (randomly) fifty names from each class (freshman, sophomore, junior, and senior). Each of these students and his or her parents are mailed a questionnaire.

_____

_____

_____

_____

_____

Exercise 5-5. Imagine that you have been hired as a consultant in the White House to help the president's staff interpret poll results. Consider the results of a NPR/*PBS NewsHour*/Marist Poll conducted between January 11 and January 13, 2019.[2] Answer the questions below based on the excerpt.

This survey of 1,023 adults was conducted January 10th through January 13th, 2019, by The Marist Poll sponsored in partnership with NPR and *PBS NewsHour*. Adults 18 years of age and older residing in the contiguous United States were contacted on landline or mobile numbers and interviewed in English by telephone using live interviewers. Mobile telephone numbers were randomly selected based upon a list of telephone exchanges from throughout the nation from Survey Sampling International. The exchanges were selected to ensure that each region was represented in proportion to its population. Mobile phones are treated as individual devices. After validation of age, personal ownership, and non-business-use of the mobile phone, interviews are typically conducted with the person answering the phone. To increase coverage, this mobile sample was supplemented by respondents reached through random dialing of landline phone numbers from Survey Sampling International. Within each landline household, a single respondent is selected through a random selection process to increase the representativeness of traditionally under-covered survey populations. Assistance was provided by Luce Research for data collection. The samples were then combined and balanced to reflect the 2017 American Community Survey 1-year estimates for age, gender, income, race, and region.

TABLE 5-1 ■ Results of NPR/*PBS NewsHour*/Marist Poll Conducted between January 11 and January 13, 2019

	Approve	Disapprove	Unsure	Sample Size	Margin of Error
National Adult	39%	53%	8%	1,023	
National Registered Voters	40%	54%	6%	873	
Latinos	50%	46%	4%	153	

a.   Complete table 5-1 by using the excerpt above, a population of 327 million Americans, and a margin of error calculator like one of these online options: https://americanresearchgroup.com/moe.html or https://www.surveymonkey.com/mp/margin-of-error-calculator/.

b.   What measures did the researchers take to assure that the survey was representative of the national population? Identify each measure and provide a short explanation about why each is important.

   1.   _____

        _____

        _____

   2.   _____

        _____

        _____

   3.   _____

        _____

        _____

   4.   _____

        _____

        _____

c.   Consider the results for Latino respondents. Your new boss is quite surprised that the level of Latino support is so high in comparison to the results for national adults and national registered voters. How would you interpret the result? What factors may explain the elevated level of support among Latinos?

   _____

   _____

   _____

   _____

   _____

   _____

   _____

   _____

Exercise 5-6.   Suppose you work in the governor's office in Maryland. You have been asked to compare the experiences of businesses owned by various ethnic groups with respect to their interaction with the state economic development office. Because all businesses must register with your state, you have a current list of all businesses and their addresses. Unfortunately, your information does not contain data about the ethnicity of the owners. You plan to send a questionnaire to a sample of business owners. Now the question of sample size comes up. Your office has limited funds but needs to make reliable inferences. Fortunately, U.S. Census Bureau data indicate the percentage of firms owned by various ethnic groups, as shown in table 5-2.

TABLE 5-2 ■ Maryland Firms by Race, 2013

Maryland Firms by Race, 2013			Expected Numbers for Samples of	
Group	Population	Percentage	200	1,000
White	361,229	68.4		
Black	101,926	19.3		
American Indian/Alaska Native	3,169	0.6		
Asian	35,912	6.8		
Hispanic	25,877	4.9		
Total	528,113	100.0		

Source: Adapted from U.S. Census Bureau, *State and County QuickFacts*, April 22, 2015, http://quickfacts.census.gov/qfd/states/24000.html.

a. If you conduct a total simple random sample of 200, what is the expected number of businesses in each ethnic group? Round to the nearest whole number. Write the numbers in the table.

b. What about a sample of 1,000? Enter these expectations in the last column.

c. Do you see any problems with the sample sizes? Explain.

_____

_____

_____

_____

_____

d. Now assume that business registration forms contained information about the ethnicity of the owners. How would you take a probability sample of 200 owners?

_____

_____

_____

_____

_____

HELPFUL HINTS

UNDERSTANDING DATA FILES

Neither the textbook nor this workbook offers much instruction in using computer software to analyze data. Many software packages are available, and political scientists have not adopted a standard. Your instructor will guide your use of the program adopted for the course.

Nevertheless, most software works the same way, and we can provide a few general tips that may be helpful for getting data into a program such as SPSS.

File extensions. Information is stored electronically in different formats. You can often tell the format by looking at the file name and especially at the *file extension,* which comprises a period and three letters. Knowing the file format lets you pick the correct program or program options when reading or opening a data file. Some common file extensions are as follows:

- **.txt** for "text" data or information. A text file contains just alphanumeric characters (for example, letters, digits, punctuation marks, a few symbols) and, when printed, looks just like something created on a typewriter or simple printer. If a program "thinks" it's reading text data, it won't recognize hidden codes for different fonts, graphics, and so forth. Consequently, if your word processor or editor (for example, NotePad) shows you a lot of gibberish, chances are that the file is not simple text. When you double-click a file name of this sort, your operating system's default word processor or editor will automatically try to open it. An example of a text file is "anes2004readme.txt," which describes a set of data pertaining to the 2004 American national election.

- **.dat** for "data." The extension does indeed suggest data, but files of this type sometimes contain alphanumeric characters as well. In either case they can be loaded into a word processor. Moreover, some statistical programs recognize the .dat extension as data and will try to open the data. SPSS, for example, reads these files. Go to "File" and then "Read Text Data." After locating the file in the menu box, the program will start a Text Import Wizard, which takes you step by step through getting the data. Examples of this format are "randomnumbers .dat," "surveytext.dat," and "surveydigits.dat." Depending on your system's configuration, double-clicking on .dat extension names will start a word processor or possibly a statistical program. But you can first run the program you want and then read the file.

- **.doc** for "document" information. This extension usually means Microsoft Word–formatted information that contains hidden formatting codes and so forth. Unless you have changed options on your computer or do not have the Windows operating system, double-clicking a .doc file will start Microsoft Word. (As we mention in the

following text, other word processors can open some versions of Word files, so you are not limited to just that package.)

- **.sav** and **.por** for SPSS data files. These file extensions "belong" to SPSS. Like most statistical software programs, SPSS allows you to give descriptive names to variables and their individual values and to create new variables or transform and recode variables in all sorts of ways. All this auxiliary information, along with the raw data, can then be saved in one file so that it is available for reuse at a later time. The file extension .sav stands for "saved." SPSS data dictionary information can be saved in a slightly more general format called .por for "portable." (We frequently use this option.) These files can be read by SPSS running on operating systems like Unix. An example is "surveydigits.por."

File structure and size. The file structure we use is quite simple: Data are presented and stored in rectangular arrays in which each row represents a case (an individual, for instance), and the columns contain values of the variables. So, if a file has 1,000 cases and two variables, the data structure is a 1,000-by-2 rectangular array of cells. Each cell holds a value for a specific case for a specific variable. (To save space on the printed page, we sometimes use "unstacked" columns.) The "surveydigits.dat" file, for example, has five columns of identification numbers and five columns of responses to make a 1,000-by-10-column matrix. But we arranged the numbers this way purely for convenience. Most software lets you stack columns on top of one another. Therefore, if you wanted, you could stack the columns 1, 3, 5, 7, and 9 of "surveydigits.dat" on top of each other and do the same with columns 2, 4, 6, 8, 10, to make a 5,000-by-2 array. Also notice that files with more than, say, thirty variables need more than one line when shown on a monitor or printed on an average piece of paper. For these data sets, the lines will "wrap" around, making them difficult to read. Finally, if you are thinking about copying a file, you can roughly estimate the file's size by multiplying the number of variables by the number of cases.

File delimiters. Most of the time the data points are separated by simple blank spaces. Occasionally, however, data are separated by tabs. (In many systems the tab character is denoted by ^t— that is, a caret and lowercase *t.*) Sometimes you have to keep this in mind when using certain software, but many times a program will detect the tabs automatically.

Case ID numbers. Some data files have explicit identification numbers for each case (for example, "surveytext.dat" and "surveydigits.dat"). In others the case number is just the row number. When you view the data matrix in a program, you will be able to determine which is the case.

Note: Our Web site (https://edge.sagepub.com/johnson9e) contains all the data files.

Exercise 5-7.   Imagine that you are working on a research project at your school on student attitudes. You are interested in measuring how responsive administrators are to issues raised by the student body through its student government using a probability sample. Assuming that your population of interest includes every enrolled student at the school, how might you build a sampling frame *without asking for or using a complete list of enrolled students*? In answering this question, think about the information that is publicly available to you and about different methods of drawing a sample.

a.   How would you build your sampling frame?

_____

_____

_____

_____

_____

_____

b.   Consider the challenges you may face in the plan you described in part a. Will your sampling frame duplicate the population of interest? Are there portions of the population that may not be included in the sampling frame?

_____

_____

_____

_____

c.   Why is it problematic if the sampling frame is different from the population of interest?

_____

_____

_____

Exercise 5-8.   Read the following abstract from a project called "Black Oversample for the American National Election Study," by Tasha Philpot and Daron Shaw, then answer the questions below.[3]

Blacks have been somewhat relegated to the sidelines in recent years by scholars more interested in America's burgeoning Latino and Asian populations. Setting aside the unique experience and place of blacks in American history and consciousness, this is regrettable for two reasons. First, the black population is often written off as "monolithic." This has, in our view, never been true but it is an increasingly troubling myth given the growing diversity of the black population. Second, many of the political and social events of the past decade have been particularly relevant for blacks: the 2000 election controversy, redistricting after the 2000 Census, and the devastation and revelations of Hurricane Katrina. If scholars are to usefully inform the public debate on matters such as mass opinion, representation, and the role of race in politics, we need a comprehensive and reliable source of data. A black over-sample within the context of the traditional ANES is an extremely effective way to achieve this.

Although the ANES has been the dominant source of data for the classic studies of turnout, partisanship, ideology, congressional voting, and political sophistication, it has been of limited use for the study of black opinion and behavior. Our study allows scholars to examine black opinion across the wide and disparate range of the ANES core instrument, as well as yielding insight into issues that predominantly concern African Americans. Furthermore, a black over-sample facilitates attitudinal and behavioral comparisons with other racial and ethnic groups as never before.

Our approach is straight-forward: working in cooperation with the ANES team at Michigan, we have overseen the recruitment, interviewing, and data collection for an over-sample of African Americans. Based on the current specifications for the 2008 ANES pre- and post-election sample, approximately 290 black respondents are interviewed, making stand-alone analyses of black opinion, attitudes, and behavior problematic. Our study adds another 310 black respondents and uses the expanded number of primary sampling units (PSU) to obtain a larger, more representative black sub-sample. In addition, by adding 10 PSUs we are able to increase the number of black respondents from racially mixed—as opposed to predominantly black—neighborhoods.

This 2008 ANES black over-sample constitutes a substantial "public good": it significantly enhances our ability to gauge the range, diversity, and determinants of African-American political opinion and vote choice. Furthermore, it facilitates informed comparisons to whites and Latinos at a time when such comparisons are especially useful to our conceptions of politics and representation.

a. Why is this "over-sample" an example of the disproportionate sampling method?

_____

_____

b. Why is a disproportionate sample like this better than a simple random sample?

_____

_____

c. Why do the authors refer to this disproportionate sample as a "public good?"

_____

_____

_____

Exercise 5-9.   You are working for a nonprofit agency based in New York that is trying to encourage political mobilization in South Africa. The organization plans to interview South Africans about attitudes toward participation and elections before developing a plan of action. In the space below, discuss the advantages and disadvantages of using a cluster sample.

_____

_____

_____

_____

_____

NOTES

1. Laura Beth Nielsen, "Situating Legal Consciousness: Experiences and Attitudes of Ordinary Citizens about Law and Street Harassment," *Law and Society Review* 34, no. 4 (2000): 1055–90. Reprinted with permission of John Wiley & Sons, Inc.

2. Full results are available online at http://maristpoll.marist.edu/wp-content/uploads/2019/01/NPR_PBS-NewsHour_Marist-Poll-USA-NOS-and-Tables_1901141631-1.pdf.

3. Tasha Philpot and Daron Shaw, "Black Oversample for the American National Election Study," *Grantome*, http://grantome.com/grant/NSF/SES-0752987. Reprinted with permission of the authors.

6 RESEARCH DESIGN: ESTABLISHING CAUSATION

Making Causal Inferences

The goal in chapter 6 of the textbook is to introduce causation. We began the chapter by showing what is necessary to demonstrate causality and explaining how hard it is to do so. We then demonstrated the logic of causation and how political scientists establish causation using the classic random experiment. In addition, we explored how both qualitative and quantitative methods can be used to demonstrate causation.

In this workbook chapter, you will focus on reinforcing your understanding of causation and causal relationships. Most of the following assignments call for serious thought rather than paper-and-pencil calculations. The purpose is to ensure that some of the basic ideas are clearly understood. We do not expect that most students will be able to design and carry out a major empirical research project. At the same time, it is important to understand how systematic and rigorous research proceeds.

Exercise 6-1. Sometimes political science students can be confused by similar-sounding terms. This confusion is often exacerbated when it comes to the methodological terms you will find in this chapter. For each of the word pairs below, define each term and then explain the important differences between them.

a. Internal validity and external validity

_____

_____

_____

b. Causation and correlation

_____

_____

_____

c. Experimental effect and experimental group

_____

_____

_____

d. Test factor and pretest

_____

_____

_____

e. Causes of effects approach and effects of causes approach

_____

_____

_____

HELPFUL HINTS
UNDERSTANDING CAUSATION

While correlation simply means that two or more variables covary, causation incorporates theoretical explanation. Remember that there are three important components in establishing causation:

1. **Covariation.** It demonstrates that the alleged cause (call it X) does in fact covary with the supposed effect (call it Y). Public opinion polls or surveys can relatively easily identify associations. To make a causal inference, however, more is needed.

2. **Time order.** The research must demonstrate that the cause preceded the effect: X must come before Y in time. After all, can an effect appear before its cause? In many observational settings, it may be difficult, if not impossible, to tell whether X came before or after Y. Still, even if we can be confident of the time order, we have to demonstrate that a third condition holds.

3. **Elimination of possible alternative causes, sometimes termed _confounding factors_.** The research must be conducted in such a way that all possible joint causes of X and Y have been eliminated.

Exercise 6-2.   In this exercise you will think about the nature of causal and spurious relationships. Figure 6-1 in the textbook demonstrates a causal relationship and a spurious relationship between celebrity endorsement and voting. Can you apply causal and spurious relationships to a different topic?

For example, consider the relationship between foreign direct investment (FDI) and the stability of authoritarian regimes. Bak and Moon have hypothesized that increases in FDI can be used by authoritarian leaders to reduce the likelihood of experiencing political challenges from elites.[1] The logic is that increases in FDI provide a greater pool of resources an authoritarian leader can divide among political elites. Dividing these resources among elites serves as a way to increase regime stability because the resources can buy the tacit support of those who might otherwise serve as challengers to the regime.

Think about the hypothesized causal relationship. In the space following, draw two different diagrams: one diagram that represents the hypothesized causal relationship between FDI and regime stability, and a second diagram that represents a spurious relationship between FDI and regime stability. Make sure to provide a short explanation of each diagram.

a. Causal relationship:

_____

_____

_____

_____

b. Explanation for causal relationship diagram: _____

_____

_____

_____

_____

c. Spurious relationship:

d. Explanation for spurious relationship diagram: _____

_____

_____

_____

_____

Exercise 6-3. Imagine that your professor mentions in class that most college students rely on _The Daily Show_ for political news and information. Your professor seems to think that following politics is necessary to get many of the jokes but that no one really learns anything by watching the show. You have decided to test your professor's ideas in the form of a research project for class using a classic randomized experiment.

In the space below, state the research question and hypotheses you intend to test as clearly and succinctly as possible. Next, explain how you would test these hypotheses and evaluate the strengths and weaknesses of this research strategy.

_____

_____

_____

_____

_____

_____

_____

_____

Exercise 6-4.   List the strengths and weaknesses of randomized controlled experiments. In particular, pay attention to the important concepts raised in the textbook chapter, including internal and external validity.

a.   Strengths:

_____

_____

_____

_____

_____

b.   Weaknesses:

_____

_____

_____

_____

_____

Exercise 6-5.   For this assignment you will first need to read Stephen D. Ansolabehere, Shanto Iyengar, Adam Simon, and Nicholas Valentino's article, "Does Attack Advertising Demobilize the Electorate?" *American Political Science Review* 88, no. 4 (1994): 829–38. You will want to pay special attention to the first three pages and appendix A. This exercise asks you to contemplate the authors' experimental research design and answer the questions below.

a.   What is the research question?

_____

b.   Please summarize the theory.

_____

_____

_____

c.   What is the central hypothesis the authors want to test?

_____

d.   In the literature review the authors point out limitations in previous work on this topic. What were those limitations and why are they important in terms of internal validity?

_____

_____

_____

e.   What special design features did the authors use to improve on the limitations of previous work?

_____

_____

_____

f.   How did the authors address external validity through their nonrandom sampling methods? Why is this important?

_____

_____

Exercise 6-6.   In the textbook we explain the difference between quantitative and qualitative approaches to empirical research. In the space below, explain the distinctive characteristics of the two approaches.

a.   Distinctive qualitative characteristics:

_____

_____

---

b. Distinctive quantitative characteristics:

NOTE

1. Daehee Bak and Chungshik Moon, "Foreign Direct Investment and Authoritarian Stability," *Comparative Political Studies* 49, no. 14 (2016): 1998–2037. doi:10.1177/0010414016655536

7 QUALITATIVE RESEARCH: CASE STUDY DESIGNS

In chapter 7 in the textbook, we explored qualitative research design issues focusing on the case study design—studies that focus on just one case or a small number of cases. The case study method is particularly useful for understanding rare or singular events. The chapter explored the logic of the case study design, focusing on the purpose of case studies, case selection procedures, establishing causation, and understanding the limits of generalization. The exercises in this chapter will give you opportunities to both sharpen your understanding of the case study design and also apply different kinds of case study designs and case selection procedures.

Exercise 7-1. In this exercise you will explore similar terms to sharpen your understanding. Below you will find five pairs of terms that have similar but different meanings. Define each term and explain why the terms in a pair are different.

a. Causally heterogeneous population and causally homogeneous population

_____

_____

_____

b. Hypothesis-generating case study and hypothesis-testing case study

_____

_____

_____

c. Method of agreement and method of difference

_____

_____

_____

d. Least likely case and most likely case

_____

_____

_____

e. Necessary cause and sufficient cause

_____

_____

_____

Exercise 7-2.   Political scientists use case studies for different purposes. As we discuss in the text, case study designs can be categorized by their purpose: an ideographic case study, a hypothesis-generating case study, a hypothesis-testing case study, or a plausibility probe. In this exercise you will think about the differences in these case study designs by describing how you would use each to address a similar topic:

Research topic: The rise of right-wing populist leaders

In the space below, design an ideographic case study, a hypothesis-generating case study, a hypothesis-testing case study, and a plausibility probe that would help you learn about the topic. For each case study, suggest a case or cases that you would use to investigate the rise of right-wing populist leaders and explain the objective of the study as it relates to the research topic. See the plausibility probe answer below as an example or model answer.

a. Plausibility probe

1. Case or cases: Examination of election of Jair Bolsonaro as Brazil's president

2. Objectives of design: This design will focus on one presidential election in Brazil in which a right-wing populist presidential candidate won an election. *The objective of this design is to develop and sharpen a theory of the rise of right-wing populism. As part of the theory-building process, I will look to conceptualize and operationalize key terms and consider if the Bolsonaro election is in fact a suitable test case to learn about the rise of right-wing populism. This plausibility probe will be used to make sure that this case is worthwhile before investing resources in a full-scale research project.*

b. Ideographic case study

1. Case or cases: _____

_____

_____

2. Objectives of design: _____

_____

_____

_____

_____

_____

_____

_____

_____

_____

c.   Hypothesis-generating case study

1.   Case or cases: _____

_____

_____

2.   Objectives of design: _____

_____

_____

_____

_____

_____

_____

_____

d.   Hypothesis-testing case study

1.   Case or cases: _____

_____

2.   Objectives of design: _____

_____

_____

_____

_____

_____

_____

_____

_____

Exercise 7-3.   As explained in chapter 7 of the textbook in more detail, case study research often uses the comparison of cases and logical arguments to make inferences about relationships between causes and outcomes. The comparative method is often traced back to the English philosopher John Stuart Mill, who described two comparative strategies: the method of difference and the method of agreement. Use the data in table 7-1 to select cases for a case study of democratization using the method of difference and for a case study of democratization using the method of agreement. For this study the outcome is successful transition to democracy by 1990.

In table 7-1 the process by which countries were democratizing is labeled as *transformation* (democratized when elites in power brought about democracy), *replacement* (democratized when opposition groups brought about democracy), or *transplacement* (democratized by government and opposition groups jointly).

TABLE 7-1 ■ Selected Democratizing Countries			
Country	**Regime**	**Democratization Process**	**Democracy by 1990**
Argentina	Military	Replacement	Yes
Bolivia	Military	Transplacement	Yes
East Germany	One-party	Replacement	Yes
Mexico	One-party	Transformation	No
Nepal	Personal	Transplacement	No
Spain	Personal	Transformation	Yes
Turkey	Military	Transformation	Yes
USSR	One-party	Transformation	No

Source: Huntington, Samuel P., "How Countries Democratize," *Political Science Quarterly* 106, no. 4 (Winter 1991–1992): 579–61.

a. Identify two countries you would select from the table above as cases in a study of successful transition to democracy using a *method of difference.*

_____

b. Explain why you chose the two countries identified in part a.

_____

_____

_____

c. Identify two countries you would select from the table above as cases in a study of successful transition to democracy using a *method of agreement.*

_____

d. Explain why you chose the two countries identified in part c.

_____

_____

_____

Exercise 7-4. When choosing a case for a case study, political scientists do not usually choose a case through random selection, as if generating a representative sample. Instead, researchers make a careful, purposive selection based on many important factors we discuss in the textbook. One key factor in case selection is whether the case is the *most likely case* or the *least likely case*.

For this exercise you will select a most likely case and a least likely case from the countries listed in table 7-2. You will be assessing a theory that high levels of personal and economic freedom and education cause superior economic performance as measured by GDP per capita.

The most important factor in the theory is that high levels of economic freedom cause high levels of GDP per capita.

TABLE 7-2 ■ Data for Select Countries				
Country	Personal Freedom Index Score	Expected Education in Years	Economic Freedom Index Score	GDP per Capita
Estonia	9.01	16	7.86	$31,800
Georgia	7.58	15	8.02	$10,700
Ghana	7.87	12	6.60	$4,700
Hong Kong	8.58	16	8.97	$61,400
Jordan	6.24	13	7.46	$12,500
Morocco	5.99	12	6.37	$8,600
Qatar	5.53	13	7.49	$124,500
Venezuela	5.52	14	2.88	$12,100

Sources: Cato Institute, The 2018 Human Freedom Index, https://www.cato.org/human-freedom-index-new; Central Intelligence Agency, *The World Factbook*, https://www.cia.gov/library/publications/the-world-factbook/rankorder/2004rank.html; and United Nations Development Programme, UN Human Development Index, http://hdr.undp.org/sites/default/files/hdi_table.pdf.

Notes: Personal Freedom Scale (High→6.66↗Medium↗3.33→Low)

Economic Freedom Scale (High→6.66↗Medium↗3.33→Low)

Education Scale (High→15↗Medium↗14→Low)

GDP Per Capita (High→$55,000↗Medium↗$35,000→Low)

a. Most likely case: Remember that a most likely case is one in which theory predicts an outcome is most likely to occur because all of the causal factors indicate that we should observe the theorized outcome.

1. Identify a most likely case from the countries listed in table 7-2.

_____

2. Explain why you chose this most likely case.

_____

_____

_____

3. What would your conclusion be if the theory failed to explain the most likely case?

_____

_____

_____

b. Least likely case: Remember that a least likely case is one where the outcome is least likely to occur because all of the causal factors except the factor of most interest predict that we will not observe the theorized outcome.

1. Identify a least likely case from the countries listed in table 7-2.

    _____

2. Explain why you chose this least likely case.

    _____

    _____

    _____

3. What would your conclusion be if the theory explained the least likely case?

    _____

    _____

    _____

c. Deviant case: Remember that a deviant case is one that exhibits all of the factors thought to lead to a particular outcome but in which the outcome does not occur.

1. Identify a deviant case from the countries listed in table 7-2.

    _____

2. Explain why you chose this deviant case.

    _____

    _____

    _____

3. How might studying this deviant case contribute to the revision and refinement of the theory?

    _____

    _____

    _____

Exercise 7-5. In this exercise you will contemplate case selection in a comparative study research design. Imagine that you are interested in studying the role nongovernmental organizations play in reducing conflict during civil war. You might begin by limiting your scope to intrastate conflict in the 1990s. You can find a list of such conflicts in table 7-3. Unfortunately for humankind, it is a very long list. As you have limited resources (time during a busy semester being the most pressing), you will use a comparative study

TABLE 7-3 ■ Intrastate Conflicts in the 1990s				
War Name	Began	Ended	Deaths	Continent
Rwanda vs. Tutsi	9/30/90	8/4/93	2,000	Africa
Sierra Leone vs. RUF	3/23/91	4/23/96	20,000	Africa
Yugoslavia/Serbia vs. Croatians	5/1/91	1/3/92	10,000	Europe
Turkey vs. Kurds	7/10/91		28,000	Middle East
Burundi vs. Tutsi Supremacists	11/23/91	12/31/91	3,000	Africa
Georgia vs. Gamsakurdia & Abkaz	12/25/91	5/14/94	3,000	Europe
Azerbaijan vs. Nagorno-Karabakh	12/25/91	7/27/94	3,250	Europe
Bosnia/Herzogovina vs. Serbs	3/3/92	11/21/95	1,359	Europe
Algeria vs. Islamic Rebels	2/7/92		80,000	Middle East
Tadzhikistan vs. Popular Democratic Army	5/1/92	6/27/97	20,000	Asia
Liberia vs. NPFL & ULIMO	10/15/92	8/19/95	150,000	Africa
Angola vs. UNITA of 1992	10/28/92	11/22/94	100,000	Africa
Zaire vs. Rebels	1/28/93	2/4/93	1,000	Africa
Burundi vs. Hutu of 1993	10/21/93		200,000	Africa
Cambodia vs. Khmer Rouge of 1993	1/29/93	7/1/97	15,000	Asia
Russia vs. Chechens	12/11/94	4/30/96	30,000	Europe
Rwanda vs. Patriotic Front	4/6/94	7/18/94	500,000	Africa
Yemen vs. South Yemen	2/21/94	7/7/94	7,000	Middle East
Pakistan vs. Mohajir	11/4/94	12/31/95	2,000	Asia
Uganda vs. Lords Resistance Army	2/8/96		10,000	Africa
Liberia vs. National Patriotic Forces	4/5/96	8/20/96	3,000	Africa
Iraq vs. KDP Kurds	8/31/96	9/7/96	1,500	Middle East
Zaire vs. Kabila-ADFL	10/8/96	5/17/97	1,000	Africa
Congo vs. Denis Sassou Nguemo	6/5/97	10/15/97	4,000	Africa

Source: Adapted from the Correlates of War Project, COW War Data 1816-2017 (v4.0) via Globalsecurity.org, https://www.globalsecurity.org/military/world/war/20th-century4.htm.

Note: Conflicts without an "Ended" date should be treated as an active conflict.

research design and limit your exploration through case selection. You have decided that, based on your schedule, you will only have time to compare three cases.

a. Which three conflicts would you choose from the list?

1. _____

2. _____

3. _____

b. Why did you choose these three cases? Did you choose cases that were similar or different in some way? Were you concerned about a particular region of the globe? What about the length of the conflicts or the number of casualties? Please explain your rationale for case selection in detail.

_____

_____

_____

_____

_____

_____

_____

_____

_____

HELPFUL HINTS
THE IMPORTANCE OF CASE SELECTION

There are many differences between qualitative and quantitative work, but the importance of case selection is not one of them. Whether you choose a qualitative or quantitative project, or whether you choose a random or nonrandom case selection method, case selection is critical. Recall that in chapter 5 of the textbook we discussed that the advantage of random sampling is that when every unit in a well-defined population has an equal chance of selection, the resulting sample is likely to be more representative of the population than if another sampling method is used, allowing for generalization from the sample to the population. A sloppy random sampling process, however, can lead to bias and poor inferences because the sample is not representative of the population. Likewise, in chapter 7 we discussed how the choice of case for a case study is instrumental in making conclusions. Conclusions drawn in a case study rely directly on the case or cases chosen. If case selection is made in haste or fails to consider relevant case characteristics, the conclusions will be less useful than if case selection is done with more care. Because a case study relies heavily on a few cases or just one case, the case selection process is of utmost importance.

Exercise 7-6.   Process tracing is an important tool in the qualitative researcher's tool box. Process tracing uses deductive reasoning to determine the process leading to an outcome and whether the explanation is true. In chapter 7 in the textbook, we reviewed four tests Stephen Van Evera identified to evaluate evidence in a process and make deductive conclusions: hoop tests, smoking gun tests, doubly decisive tests, and straw-in-wind tests. In this exercise you will first provide a definition of each test in the context of the murder example in the textbook. After defining the tests, you will complete a logical table that locates the tests on the necessary and sufficient conditions.

a. Review the process-tracing section in chapter 7 of the textbook to refresh your memory of the murder case. In that example we were evaluating the hypothesis that a suspect shot a victim. Table 7-4 includes the four tests as well as three additional columns:

evidence, unique, and certain. The evidence column includes the evidence that led the suspect to pass each test. In the remaining columns, indicate if the test is unique or certain by writing yes or no.

(*Hint:* Tests of evidence vary to the extent to which they make unique or certain predictions. Evidence needs to be tested for its usefulness in reaching conclusions. Stephen Van Evera points out that a strong test of a hypothesis is one in which evidence is *uniquely* predicted by a theory and is *certain* or unequivocal in the prediction.)

TABLE 7-4 ■ Data for Select Countries			
Test	Evidence	Unique (Yes/No)	Certain (Yes/No)
Straw-in-the-wind:	Sale of business		
Hoop:	In vicinity		
Smoking gun:	Powder residue		
Doubly decisive:	CCTV footage		

Next we can consider how process tracing can be used to test for causal inferences. Table 7-5 below will help you contemplate how process-tracing tests can be used to test for causal inferences. The column heading in the table is *Sufficient Causes* with two options, *No* or *Yes*. The row heading in the table is *Necessary Causes* with two options, *No* or *Yes*. How can you complete the table with the four process-tracing tests discussed in the textbook: hoop tests, smoking gun tests, doubly decisive tests, and straw-in-the-wind tests?

b. Complete the table by adding each of the four tests—hoop tests, smoking gun tests, doubly decisive tests, and straw-in-the-wind tests—to the four empty cells in the table. Each test can only be used once in one of the four empty cells. While completing table 7-5, think about the nature of unique and certain evidence as it relates to necessary and sufficient causes.

(*Hint:* Remember that a necessary cause is a condition that *must be present* in order for the outcome to occur. The presence of a necessary condition does not guarantee an outcome: A condition *may be necessary but not sufficient.*)

TABLE 7-5 ■ Necessary and Sufficient Causes			
		Sufficient Causes	
		No	Yes
Necessary	No		
Causes	Yes		

c. Why did you place the tests as you did? Explain your logic for each cell.

1. Not necessary/not sufficient:

   _____

   _____

2. Not necessary/sufficient:

   _____

   _____

3. Necessary/not sufficient:

_____

_____

4. Necessary/sufficient:

_____

_____

Exercise 7-7.   It is important to consider the difference between a causally homogenous population and a causally heterogencous population. Recall from chapter 7 in the textbook that "a _causally homogeneous population_ is 'one in which a given cause can be expected to have the _same_ causal relationship with the outcome across cases in the population,' whereas a _causally heterogeneous population_ is 'one where a given cause might have many different effects across different cases or the same cause is linked to the same outcome through different causal mechanisms.'"

Consider the two case selection processes below. One is an example of a causally homogenous population and the other is an example of a causally heterogeneous population. Label each with the appropriate population.

a. First Case Selection Process

Research question	What are the causes of interstate conflict?
Interstate conflict definition:	An interstate conflict is any military engagement between two or more countries that results in more than fifty deaths in a calendar year.
Case selection:	All military engagements that resulted in more than fifty deaths in a calendar year are included in the population for analysis.
Causally homogenous population or causally heterogenous population?	Causally _____ population

b.   Second Case Selection Process

Research question	What are the causes of interstate conflict?
Interstate conflict definition:	An interstate conflict is any military engagement that results in more than 50,000 deaths in a calendar year.
Case selection:	All military engagements that resulted in more than 50,000 deaths in a calendar year are included in the population for analysis.
Causally homogenous population or causally heterogenous population?	Causally _____ population

c. Explain why you labeled each case selection process as a causally homogenous population or causally heterogenous population.

_____

_____

_____

_____

_____

_____

_____

_____

8 MAKING EMPIRICAL OBSERVATIONS
Qualitative Analysis

Observation of political activities and behaviors is a data collection method that can be used profitably by political scientists. In chapter 8 of the textbook, we discussed various observation methods for data collection. We discussed three methods—interviews, document analysis, and direct observation—and focused on how these data collection methods are used in qualitative research studies. Political scientists choose among data collection methods based on their resources, their research question, the properties of different collection methods, and many other factors.

In the exercises below, you will have opportunities to think about the many choices political scientists make when it comes to data collection. You will be asked to apply different data collection methods in order to become more familiar with each method and also so you can experience firsthand some of the difficulties researchers face in data collection.

Exercise 8-1.   In the first exercise in this chapter, you will focus on key terms in the core text. For each pair of terms, provide a definition and explain the difference between the terms.

a.   Accretion measures and erosion measures

_____

_____

_____

b.   Direct observation and indirect observation

_____

_____

_____

c.   Episodic records and running records

_____

_____

_____

d.   Primary data and secondary data

_____

_____

_____

Exercise 8-2.   David A. Bositis noted in his article, "Some Observations on the Participant Method," *Political Behavior* 10 (Winter 1988): 333–48, that "a key feature of participant observation design is an ability to both observe behavior and to provoke behaviors to be subsequently observed." Read Bositis's article and think of situations in which your participation (either your physical presence or verbal communication) could provoke behaviors to be observed. Are any ethical considerations raised by these situations? If not, think of a situation that poses some ethical issues. If all of the situations you thought of pose ethical issues, try to think of one that does *not* raise ethical issues. Write your ideas below.

_____

_____

_____

_____

_____

_____

_____

_____

Exercise 8-3.   Read Laura Beth Nielsen's article, "Situating Legal Consciousness: Experiences and Attitudes of Ordinary Citizens about Law and Street Harassment," *Law and Society Review* 34, no. 4 (2000): 1055–90, especially the "Method" section beginning on page 1061. (You can find the excerpt in this workbook in chapter 5, exercise 5-3.) How did observation play a role in Nielsen's research?

_____

_____

_____

_____

_____

_____

_____

_____

Exercise 8-4.   Read James M. Glaser's article, "The Challenges of Campaign Watching: Seven Lessons of Participant-Observation Research," *PS: Political Science and Politics* 29 (September 1996): 533–37. Why is participant observation important to studying political campaigns? How important is flexibility in this type of research?

_____

_____

_____

_____

_____

_____

Exercise 8-5.   This exercise will allow you to put your participant observation skills to the test by attending a local gathering. Ideally you will attend a political meeting of some kind, such as a city council meeting or a political party meeting, but any kind of gathering will allow you to practice these skills. First, develop a hypothesis about the behavior you will witness. You might want to think about how elected officials will interact with each other, how citizens attending the gathering will behave, or simply how people will observe social conventions. Or you might have ideas about the kinds of issues citizens will discuss, such as local ordinances, requests for services, or complaints about a problem in the community. You can hypothesize about almost anything that is appropriate for the gathering you choose.

a.   Write your hypothesis on the line below.

_____

b.   Which gathering did you attend?

_____

c.   After attending the gathering, what observations did you make that contributed to testing your hypothesis?

_____

_____

_____

_____

_____

_____

d.   Based on your observations, was your hypothesis correct? Why or why not?

_____

_____

HELPFUL HINTS
BE CAREFUL WHEN OBSERVING THE PUBLIC

In chapter 8 of the textbook, we discussed several ways to make direct and indirect observations. In general, and especially if you are working through a university or college, you must obtain the informed consent of individuals you question in a poll or survey or use in an experiment. Getting this agreement may be a straightforward matter of asking for permission, which subjects should feel completely free to give or deny. You may, however, be involved in direct or indirect observation of people (or their possessions) that does not involve face-to-face contact. (Suppose, for example, you want to observe a protest march.) Even in this case you should adopt some standards of responsible and courteous research:

- Be aware of your personal safety. Make sure someone knows where you are going. Carry proper identification. It also would not hurt to carry a letter of introduction from your professor, supervisor, or employer.

- Depending on the nature of the study, it may be wise to contact local authorities to tell them that you will be in a certain area collecting data in a particular way. If you seem to be just hanging around a neighborhood, park, or schoolyard, you could possibly be reported as someone acting suspiciously.

- Always ask permission if you enter private property. If no one is available to give permission, come back

later or try somewhere else. Even in many public accommodations, such as arenas or department stores, you will probably need to get prior approval to do your research.

- Respect people's privacy even when they are in public places.

- Do not misrepresent yourself. Some of our students once had an issue with this. They wanted to compare the treatment that whites and nonwhites received in rural welfare offices. They pretended to be needy and applied for public assistance in order to observe the behavior of welfare officers. By doing this, however, they were breaking state and federal laws. They got off with a warning, but it is always a big mistake to fake being someone you are not just to collect data.

- Be willing, even eager, to share your results with those who have asked about your activities. Volunteer to send them a copy of your study. (Doing so will encourage cooperation.)

- When observing a demonstration, protest march, debate, or similar confrontation, do not appear to take sides.

Exercise 8-6.   Some direct observation research takes place in a laboratory where researchers can carefully control conditions, such as the number of participants, the physical environment, stimuli, etc. Other observation takes place in a natural setting where researchers have no control but can observe real interactions. Sometimes observation is used to test hypotheses, and in other cases observation is used to generate hypotheses. In this exercise you will make observations in a natural setting using streaming video of a U.S. Senate committee hearing. Your task is to develop hypotheses about how elected officials interact with witnesses. Although the hearing is from long ago (1969!), you should find the interaction between the witness and the senator engaging to watch.

a.   Watch the six-minute excerpt of the Senate Committee on Commerce hearing on the Public Broadcasting Act of 1967 at www .americanrhetoric.com/speeches/fredrogerssenatetestimonypbs.htm. List your observations on the interaction between Senator Pastore and the witness, Fred Rogers. These observations might be about speaking tone, number of interruptions, speech content, or many other concepts related to the interaction between political actors. You may find the transcript of the video clip useful in making observations as well.[1]

b.   Record your observations in the space below.

_____

_____

_____

_____

_____

c. List three hypotheses you could test about the interaction between elected officials and witnesses based on your observations.

_____

_____

_____

Exercise 8-7.   As you have proven yourself to be a careful researcher by doing well in this course, your professor has hired you to work on a project on UN Security Council procedures. The project is in its nascent stages, and your professor would like you to study Security Council meetings, make observations, and report on important procedural details. Your first assignment is to watch an archived UN Security Council video from 1993 in regard to violence in Cambodia. You will find the archived video at https://www .unmultimedia.org/avlibrary/asset/2346/2346955/. In addition to the video, you will find the referenced statement at https://undocs .org/en/S/PV.3230. You can make observations of the video, the text, or both. Your professor requires ten observations about UN Security Council procedure. The first two observations below will give you examples of the sorts of things you can expect to observe. After you record each observation, indicate why you think the observation may be important.

a. Observation:

The Security Council provided video dubbed in English for the speech delivered in Spanish and made the written statement available in English.

Importance:
I can probably expect to find most materials produced in English no matter what language the speaker uses.

b. Observation:

The president of the Security Council read the statement before the council.

Importance:
The committee may have rules about who reads statements on behalf of the council.

c. Observation:

_____

_____

_____

Importance:

_____

_____

_____

d. Observation:

_____

_____

_____

Importance:

_____

_____

_____

e. Observation:

_____

_____

_____

Importance:

_____

_____

_____

f. Observation:

_____

_____

_____

Importance:

_____

_____

_____

g. Observation:

_____

_____

_____

Importance:

_____

_____

_____

h. Observation:

_____

_____

_____

Importance:

_____

_____

_____

i. Observation:

_____

_____

_____

Importance:

_____

_____

_____

j. Observation:

_____

_____

_____

Importance:

_____

_____

_____

Exercise 8-8.   Imagine that you are interested in studying how people collect and use political information when making a decision. You are particularly interested in how much information people feel they need to make an informed decision. You want to test the hypothesis that people will seek to collect more information before making a decision when it is easy to collect information. For this exercise assume that you have access to a suitable laboratory space with top-of-the-line audio and video equipment for recording behavior and a representative sample of willing participants. You can also feel free to spend a great deal of virtual money to create the ultimate observational design. (*Hint:* You should begin by identifying the decision that participants must make. Remember also that you will need to assess how people make use of easy-to-find information and hard-to-find information. How can you make information easy or hard to find?)

a.   In the space below, describe how you could use a laboratory setting to test this hypothesis through direct observation.

_____

_____

_____

_____

_____

_____

_____

b.   In the space below, explain why you chose to design your observational study in this way. Why might observation in a laboratory be better than in a natural setting to test a hypothesis like this?

_____

_____

_____

_____

_____

Exercise 8-9.   The goal of ethnography is to make cultural interpretations through personal observation of everyday life. In order to make these interpretations, researchers immerse themselves in the community under study. As a student you are in a position to make direct observations of political life on campus. In this exercise you will make direct observations of how the campus community embraces recycling efforts. Most colleges and universities have recycling programs in place and encourage members of the campus community to recycle. For this exercise you should find a spot in a cafeteria at your school where you can observe a garbage bin and a recycling bin in near proximity—ideally next to each other. If you are off campus, you can find a similar location at a busy public location. For a short period (twenty to thirty minutes) during a busy time in the cafeteria, such as lunch or dinner, make observations about how members of the campus community embrace recycling. Do people recycle? Are they using each bin as intended? Do some people carefully divide trays into multiple bins? Do some people remind their friends to recycle? Are there recycling instructions posted near the bin? Are there recycling instructions posted elsewhere in the building?

a. Make your observations on the lines below. Indicate when, where, and for how long you made these observations.

_____

_____

_____

_____

_____

_____

_____

_____

_____

b. What interpretations can you make about the recycling movement at your school based on these observations?

_____

_____

_____

_____

c. How might you gain a better understanding of recycling as a social norm of behavior at your school? What other kinds of observations might be necessary?

_____

_____

_____

NOTE

1. Extension of Authorizations under the Public Broadcasting Act of 1967, Hearings, 91st Cong., 1st sess., on S. 1242, April 30 and May 1, 1969, Washington, DC, U.S. Government Printing Office, 1969; Y 4.C 73/2: 91-5.

QUANTITATIVE RESEARCH DESIGNS

Chapter 9 in the textbook is a companion to chapter 7. While chapter 7 explored qualitative research and the use of case studies, chapter 9 explored quantitative research and the use of experimental designs beyond the classic random experiment and quantitative observational designs. There are of course many kinds of experiments beyond the classic random experiment, including posttest only, repeated measurement, multigroup, field, and natural experiments. The chapter also discussed observational designs, such as cross-sectional and longitudinal designs. In this chapter in the workbook, you will get a chance to apply these different methods in the exercises. You will also think about why researchers choose to use these methods and consider the key differences between them.

Exercise 9-1. For each pair of terms below, define each term and explain how the terms are different.

a. Cross-sectional design and longitudinal design

_____

_____

_____

b. Field experiment and natural experiment

_____

_____

_____

c. Age effects and cohort

_____

_____

_____

d. Posttest design and repeated measurement design

_____

_____

_____

Exercise 9-2. In chapter 9 of the textbook, we discussed a number of experimental designs that deviate from the classical randomized experiment, including the posttest design, the repeated measures design, the multigroup design, the field experiment, and the natural experiment. Each of these designs follows the same basic logic of the classical randomized experiment—measuring a reaction to a treatment. Below you will find five sample abstracts describing experimental designs. Based on the components present in each design, decide which of the following types of experiments best describe each design: multigroup design, posttest design, repeated measurement design, field experiment, or natural experiment.

a. Type of experiment that best describes the following design: _____

   We conducted a study on the effects of mobilization on political participation among rural Mexican voters. Does preelection contact increase voter turnout among Mexicans who live in rural municipalities? Prior to the July 1, 2018, general election, we randomly selected subjects from registered voter lists and subsequently assigned those selected to a treatment group (contacted by telephone) and a control group (not contacted). A few days before Election Day, subjects in the treatment group received a phone call encouraging them to vote, while those in the control group were not contacted. After the election we compared voter turnout records for the treatment and control groups to test our hypothesis.

b. Type of experiment that best describes the following design: _____

   We are interested in the link between political debates and political knowledge. We used an availability sample of 100 undergraduate students enrolled in an introductory political science class. The students were randomly assigned to a treatment group that watched a political debate and a control group that watched a Hallmark original holiday movie. After watching the debate or movie, the students completed a posttest that asked factual knowledge questions about the candidates participating in the debate. We then compared the posttest scores between the treatment and control groups to test our hypothesis.

c. Type of experiment that best describes the following design: _____

   We want to know if civics classes can successfully build support for democracy. In 1994 Poland introduced school programs to build support for democracy in many, but not all, schools. In 1995 we distributed surveys to 500 randomly chosen students in schools where students had taken a mandatory civics course during the previous school year (the civics treatment group). We also distributed surveys to 500 randomly chosen students in schools that did not offer a civics course and students therefore had not taken a civics course during the previous school year (the control group). To test our hypothesis, we compared the scores between the treatment and control groups.

d. Type of experiment that best describes the following design: _____

   We are interested in how long political motivation lasts. We recruited subjects using an availability sample of voting-age adults. Participants were given a pretest focused on political motivation when they arrived at our testing facility. After the pretest we introduced a motivational speaker who gave an inspiring talk on the importance of social justice. After the talk the participants answered posttest questions about political motivation. Participants then spent thirty minutes making social justice–themed posters. The participants then returned each day for the following week to spend a half hour each day making more posters, and each day they also completed the same posttest focusing on political motivation so that we could measure the lasting effect of political motivation.

e. Type of experiment that best describes the following design: _____

   We are interested in understanding the circumstances under which citizens decide to make a campaign donation. We created a random sample drawn from voter registration data of 200 voting-age citizens who identify with the Republican Party. Each participant was promised $50 for participating and was assigned to the control group or one of three treatment groups. Participants in each group were asked to read a short article about the Republican candidate for governor. The article for the control group did not include any information about the candidate's campaign finance circumstances. Each of the treatment groups read the same article, but a different section was added for each treatment group. The first treatment group read that the Republican had about the same amount of money as her Democratic opponent. The second treatment group read that the Republican had 10 percent less than her Democratic opponent. The third treatment group read that the Republican had 10 percent more than her Democratic opponent. Each participant then had an opportunity to donate half of his or her compensation to the Republican candidate as a campaign contribution. We compared scores across the groups to test our hypotheses.

Exercise 9-3.   How would you design an experiment using a posttest design to test the effect of listening to a campaign speech on support for a candidate?

a. Describe your posttest experiment here.

_____

_____

_____

_____

_____

_____

_____

_____

b. Why is a posttest design weaker relative to a classical experimental design in terms of establishing causation?

_____

_____

_____

_____

_____

_____

Exercise 9-4. To reinforce your understanding of field experiments, read Jidong Chen, Jennifer Pan, and Yiqing Xu's article, "Sources of Authoritarian Responsiveness: A Field Experiment in China," _American Journal of Political Science_ 60, no. 2 (2016): 383–400. After reading the article and paying special attention to the research design components, answer the questions below.

a. What is the research question?

_____

b. Summarize the theory.

_____

_____

_____

_____

_____

_____

c. What are the three central hypotheses?

_____

_____

_____

_____

_____

_____

d. Why do the authors characterize this research design as a field experiment? What are the specific design features that make this characterization true?

_____

_____

_____

_____

_____

_____

e. Describe the control condition and multiple treatment conditions and explain how the authors implemented these treatments in the experiment.

_____

_____

_____

_____

_____

f. How do the control and treatment conditions relate to the central hypotheses you identified in question c?

_____

_____

_____

g. Field experiments often face ethical challenges. What are the most important ethical issues related to this field experiment research design and how did the authors address those issues?

_____

_____

_____

_____

_____

_____

HELPFUL HINTS

GETTING STARTED WITH CROSS-SECTIONAL AND LONGITUDINAL PROJECTS

One big advantage of cross-sectional and longitudinal research designs is that there is so much data publicly available on the Internet. You can begin a project by simply visiting the United Nations at http://data.un.org and find data on every country on the planet. You could visit the U.S. Census Bureau to find data on American states at https://www.census.gov/ data.html. Exploring data made available by institutions like these can lead to a research question that can be answered by downloading data and putting your research methods skills to work. If you have limited resources to dedicate to a project, starting with well-organized and documented data is a great strategy.

Exercise 9-5.   When choosing a research design, there is usually a trade-off between internal validity (causation) and external validity (generalizability).

a. In the space below, explain why you might struggle to demonstrate internal validity with a cross-sectional design.

_____

_____

_____

_____

_____

b. In the space below, explain why cross-sectional designs typically have good external validity.

_____

_____

_____

_____

_____

_____

Exercise 9-6.   One of the most popular observational studies is the cross-sectional design. In order to strengthen your understanding of the cross-sectional design, read Stefanie Bailer, Thilo Bodenstein, and V. Finn Heinrich's article, "Explaining the Strength of Civil Society: Evidence from Cross-Sectional Data," _International Political Science Review_ 34, no. 3 (June 2013): 289–309. The answers to the questions below are found between pages 289 and 296—the cross-sectional design portion of the article.

a. What is the research question?

_____

b. The authors identify four theoretical explanations for the enhancement of civil society. Briefly identify and describe each "causal channel."

  1. _____

  _____

  _____

  2. _____

  _____

  _____

  3. _____

  _____

  _____

  4. _____

  _____

  _____

c. What is the central aim of the study?

_____

_____

_____

d. Cross-sectional studies generally use the written record as observations. The authors used data from the CIVICUS Civil Society Index Project as their observations of the dependent variable, civil society. Describe how the Civil Society Index was constructed using input from experts and advisory boards.

_____

_____

_____

_____

_____

_____

e. Listed below you will find four causal factors the authors used to explain variation in the dependent variable and thereby test theoretical hypotheses. How did the authors measure each causal factor?

1. Level of socioeconomic development

_____

_____

_____

2. Political institutions

_____

_____

_____

3. Social structure

_____

_____

_____

4. International environment

_____

_____

_____

Exercise 9-7.   To reinforce your understanding of longitudinal studies, read Timothy Hellwig's article, "Globalization and Perceptions of Policy Maker Competence: Evidence from France," *Political Research Quarterly* 60, no. 1 (March 2007): 146–58. You will want to read the first five pages of the article and then answer the following questions:

a.   What is the research question?

_____

b.   The author makes and tests three arguments. Describe the three arguments.

   1.   _____

   _____

   _____

   2.   _____

   _____

   _____

   3.   _____

   _____

   _____

c.   The author seeks to test three hypotheses. List the three hypotheses here.

   1.   _____

   _____

   2.   _____

   _____

   3.   _____

   _____

d.   Why is it important that this analysis uses longitudinal data? Why are the data from France between 1985 and 2002 particularly good longitudinal data for this analysis?

_____

_____

_____

_____

_____

_____

e. What do the two dependent variables in this study measure?

_____

_____

_____

f. There are two key independent variables in the analysis that capture components of economic globalization—trade openness and capital flows. Briefly describe each variable and indicate the sources used for the variables.

1. Independent variable 1: Trade openness _____

_____

_____

2. Independent variable 2: Capital flows _____

_____

_____

3. What are the data sources for trade openness and capital flows? _____

_____

_____

Exercise 9-8.   There are many political science research questions that could be addressed with multiple research designs. Consider, for example, the politics around climate change. One could try to explain why citizens, lawmakers, or bureaucrats hold various opinions about the causes of or solutions for climate change. One might also investigate the effectiveness of various government efforts in dealing with climate change.

a. How might you use a cross-sectional research design to study the politics of climate change? (_Hint:_ You might consider using a respondent's opinion about a climate change issue as a dependent variable.)

_____

_____

_____

_____

_____

_____

b. How might you use a longitudinal or time series research design to study the politics of climate change? (*Hint:* You might consider using a measure of the effect of climate change, such as CO_2 levels, over time as your dependent variable.)

_____

_____

_____

_____

_____

_____

_____

_____

10 QUANTITATIVE METHODS

In chapter 10 of the textbook we explored quantitative data collection methods, including content analysis and surveys. Like all of the data collection methods that we have covered in previous chapters, the devil lies in the details with content analysis and surveys. It is very easy to imagine using a survey to collect answers to a research question, but making decisions on questionnaire design issues like question wording and order can be difficult. It is easy to make decisions that bias results if one is not thoughtful and careful. The exercises in this chapter provide the opportunity to apply content analysis and survey techniques, explore the intricacies of the methods, and consider the difficult choices researchers face in these designs.

Exercise 10-1. Consider each pair of terms below. Define each term and explain the difference between the two terms.

a. Branching question and filter question

_____

_____

_____

b. Response rate and response set

_____

_____

_____

c. Single-sided question and two-sided question

_____

_____

_____

d. Closed-ended question and open-ended question

_____

_____

_____

Exercise 10-2. American presidents deliver at least one State of the Union address per year. Today the speech takes place in the U.S. House of Representatives in front of most of the nation's representatives, senators, Supreme Court justices, Cabinet officials, Joint Chiefs of Staff, and other national political figures. This was not always the case. In fact, there has been a good bit of variability in how the address has been delivered, its length, its content, and who attended it. In the questions below, you will rely on content analysis data archived by the American Presidency Project, available at www.presidency.ucsb.edu/sou.php.

a. Use data about the length of the State of the Union address to generate a hypothesis about the relationship between address type (written or spoken) and address length, measured in words. You will find the data at www.presidency.ucsb.edu/sou_words.php.

_____

_____

_____

b. Presidents often invite special guests to the State of the Union address and acknowledge those guests during the address. Use data about the guests sitting in the House Gallery during the State of the Union address to generate a hypothesis about the number of these guests. You will find the data at www.presidency.ucsb.edu/sou_gallery.php.

_____

_____

_____

c. Write a hypothesis about the proportion of male to female guests sitting in the House Gallery. For this hypothesis you will need to use your best judgment based on the listed names. You will find the data at www.presidency.ucsb.edu/sou_gallery.php.

_____

_____

_____

d. Explain why coding gender based on name alone might cause problems in making inferences if your gender count data were used in a real content analysis project.

_____

_____

_____

_____

Exercise 10-3. In this exercise (next page) you will perform a simplified content analysis. Scholarly content analyses typically include many individual documents or other sources of data. For this exercise you will try your hand at analyzing the content of just one document. In this hypothetical project, you are interested in learning about the balance between issue content and content about a party's candidates. To begin, read the following Whig Party political platform from 1844.

Resolved, That, in presenting to the country the names of Henry Clay for president, and of Theodore Frelinghuysen for vice-president of the United States, this Convention is actuated by the conviction that all the great principles of the Whig party—principles inseparable from the public honor and prosperity—will be maintained and advanced by these candidates.

Resolved, That these principles may be summed as comprising, a well-regulated currency; a tariff for revenue to defray the necessary expenses of the government, and discriminating with special reference to the protection of the domestic labor of the country; the distribution of the proceeds of the sales of the public lands; a single term for the presidency; a reform of executive usurpations;—and, generally—such an administration of the affairs of the country as shall impart to every branch of the public service the greatest practicable efficiency, controlled by a well regulated and wise economy.

Resolved, That the name of Henry Clay needs no eulogy; the history of the country since his first appearance in public life is his history; its brightest pages of prosperity and success are identified with the principles which he has upheld, as its darkest and more disastrous pages are with every material departure in our public policy from those principles.

Resolved, That in Theodore Frelinghuysen we present a man pledged alike by his revolutionary ancestry and his own public course to every measure calculated to sustain the honor and interest of the country. Inheriting the principles as well as the name of a father who, with Washington, on the fields of Trenton and of Monmouth, perilled life in the contest for liberty, and afterwards, as a senator of the United States, acted with Washington in establishing and perpetuating that liberty, Theodore Frelinghuysen, by his course as Attorney-General of the State of New Jersey for twelve years, and subsequently as a senator of the United States for several years, was always strenuous on the side of law, order, and the constitution, while as a private man, his head, his hand, and his heart have been given without stint to the cause of morals, education, philanthropy, and religion.[1]

a. How would you propose measuring the amount of the platform dedicated to the Whig Party's issue positions and the amount dedicated to the party's presidential candidate, Henry Clay? Would your recording unit be the number of words, number of sentences, number of paragraphs, or another metric? Explain your choice below.

_____

_____

_____

_____

_____

_____

b. Remember that you are interested in the balance between issue content and candidate content in platforms. This platform, and most others, includes other information as well. Do you think it would be better to record the proportion of issue content to candidate content (62 percent issue to 38 percent candidate, for example) or to record the percentage of the overall platform that each component represents (53 percent "issue," 14 percent "candidate," 33 percent "other," for example). What are the relative advantages of each strategy?

_____

_____

_____

_____

_____

_____

_____

c. Because this platform is from 1844, there may be words you do not recognize and words that may have changed meaning over time. For example, the word _egregious_ once meant "standing out from the flock," but now it has a negative connotation. If you were to undertake a content analysis of historical documents, how might you tackle the problem of what words meant at the time they were used?

_____

_____

_____

_____

d. To complicate matters, let us assume that you want to code the tone of language used to describe candidates. How might you think about coding tone? Give some examples from the words and phrases used in the platform.

_____

_____

_____

_____

_____

_____

_____

Exercise 10-4. In this exercise you will perform a simplified content analysis. Scholarly content analyses typically include many individual documents or other sources of data. You will try your hand at analyzing the content of just one video clip. Content analysis often involves identifying whether important characteristics are present or absent in a document or other form of content. In this exercise you will create a content analysis coding scheme for presidential campaign advertisements. In a real content analysis, you might use your coding scheme to code the content of dozens or hundreds of advertisements from one or more candidates in one or more elections. Here you will use your coding scheme to code just one campaign commercial. This exercise is intended to help you understand how a coding scheme is used in a content analysis and make you aware of the difficulties researchers face in creating a coding scheme and coding content.

a. Your first task is to list five important characteristics about campaign commercials on the lines below. You might consider a number of characteristics, such as the type of commercial (issue oriented, biographical, attack, or negative); the use of sound or music; whether the candidate or the opposition physically appears in the ad; or even the use of footnotes for claims.

_____

_____

b. Explain how you could measure the presence of each of the characteristics you identified in part a. For example, consider the characteristic, "Candidate spoke in ad." You could watch an ad and record a 1 on a spreadsheet if the candidate spoke in the ad or a 0 if the candidate did not.

_____

_____

_____

_____

_____

_____

_____

_____

c. Using the Obama ad, "This Is a Clear Choice," from the 2012 presidential election, apply your coding scheme and record the results below. You can find the ad clip at www.livingroomcandidate.org/commercials/2012. You might also find this transcript useful.

> *Clinton:* This election, to me, is about which candidate is more likely to return us to full employment. This is a clear choice. The Republican plan is to cut more taxes on upper-income people and go back to deregulation. That's what got us in trouble in the first place. President Obama has a plan to rebuild America from the ground up. Investing in innovation, education, and job training. It only works if there is a strong middle class. That's what happened when I was president. We need to keep going with his plan.
>
> *Obama:* I'm Barack Obama and I approve this message.

_____

_____

_____

_____

_____

d. Having used your coding scheme just once, reflect on how you might improve it if you were to apply it to hundreds of ads. How would you improve your coding scheme? Why would you make these changes?

_____

_____

_____

_____

_____

_____

_____

_____

Example 10-5. For this exercise you will consider how you might use the running record to explore ideas about public policy. Imagine that you are interested in writing a research paper on climate change in Western Europe. Table 10-1 includes data from the United Nations on carbon dioxide emissions in fifteen Western European countries.

a. Complete the rest of the table by finding the population for each country. You will find population data at http://data.un.org/Data.aspx?d=POP&f=tableCode%3a22. Note that population would be best measured in 2016.

b. How might you use this data to test ideas about climate change? In the space below, generate a hypothesis about climate change using the data in table 10-1.

_____

_____

_____

TABLE 10-1 ■ Western European Carbon Dioxide Emissions, 2016		
Country	**CO$_2$ Emissions, Gigatons**	**Population**
Austria	67,402	
Belgium	100,244	
Denmark	38,427	
France	346,790	
Germany	801,753	
Ireland	39,928	
Italy	350,323	
Liechtenstein	148	
Luxembourg	9,003	
Monaco	67	
Netherlands	165,522	
Portugal	50,285	
Spain	260,986	
Switzerland	39,205	
United Kingdom	398,033	

Source: United Nations, "Carbon Dioxide (CO$_2$) Emissions without Land Use, Land-Use Change and Forestry (LULUCF), in Gigagrams (Gg)," 2016.

c. What additional data would you want to collect from the running record to test more ideas about climate change? Explore the data sets available from the United Nations at http://data.un.org/DataMartInfo.aspx, or search for United Nations data using a Web browser. List four variables or data sets you would find useful and explain why.

_____

_____

_____

_____

_____

_____

_____

_____

Exercise 10-6. Provide a short evaluation or critique of the following survey questions. If you do not see any problems with a question, just say so.

a. "What is your opinion of the proposed missile defense system? Do you oppose or favor it?"

_____

_____

_____

_____

b. "When talking with citizens, we find that most of them oppose increasing income taxes for the middle class. How about you? Would you favor or oppose an increase in income taxes for the middle class?"

_____

_____

_____

_____

c. "Would you favor or oppose a program that improved child health care?"

_____

_____

_____

_____

d. "Since the September 11, 2001, attacks in New York City and Washington, D.C., there has been a great deal of attention paid to terrorism. Do you support increased spending to protect the nation from terrorism?"

_____

_____

_____

_____

e. "Have you ever committed a felony, and if so, what did you do?"

_____

_____

_____

_____

Exercise 10-7.   Sometimes it is difficult to write high-quality survey questions that are both reliable and valid (see chapters 5 and 10 in the textbook). It is particularly important to consider content validity (whether you have fully captured the meaning of a concept with a survey question). In this exercise you are to provide a definition for each of the terms listed, write a survey question for each, and explain how each question captures the full meaning of the term.

a. Employment status

_____

_____

_____

_____

b. Attitude toward female officeholders

_____

_____

_____

_____

c. Level of support for the British prime minister

_____

_____

_____

_____

d. Political ideology

_____

_____

_____

_____

e. Level of participation in politics

_____

_____

_____

_____

Exercise 10-8. The Pew Research Center has administered over 480,000 interviews in ninety-one different countries as of 2015, mostly as part of their Global Attitudes and Religion and Public Life projects. These projects are valuable in part because they ask the same questions of people in different parts of the world across time, allowing researchers to measure differences in attitudes among people from different cultures. Survey questions might be translated into eighty or more languages, which requires a great deal of work. According to Pew,

> Translation is a multi-step process. For questions asked on earlier surveys, the center relies on translations used in previous questionnaires in order to maintain comparability of survey data over time. For new questions, Pew Research staff begin by submitting the questions to professional linguists. The linguists evaluate each question for ease of translation and make recommendations to guide proper translation. New questions, along with the linguists' recommendations, are then submitted to local research organizations, which translate the items into the appropriate language(s). Once translations are complete, they are again reviewed by professional linguists, who provide feedback to the translators. Pew Research Center staff are consulted regarding any serious debates about translation, and the center issues final approval of the translated survey instrument prior to fieldwork.[2]

a. Why does Pew use such a complicated process—involving linguists, local research organizations, and translators—to translate questions? How could the translation process affect survey responses?

_____

_____

_____

_____

_____

_____

b. Why is it important that Pew uses the same translations of questions over time? Why not revise translations when questions are reused?

_____

_____

_____

_____

_____

_____

Pew also notes that

Pew Research Center staff are responsible for the overall design and execution of each cross-national survey project, including topical focus, questionnaire development, countries to be surveyed and sample design. The center's staff frequently contract with a primary vendor to identify local, reputable research organizations, which are hired to translate questionnaires, administer surveys in the field and process data. Both primary vendors and local research organizations are consulted on matters of sampling, fieldwork logistics and translation. In addition, Pew Research often seeks the advice of subject matter experts and experienced survey researchers regarding the design and content of its cross-national studies.[3]

a. Why is it important that Pew consults with local research organizations about sampling and fieldwork in foreign countries?

_____

_____

_____

_____

_____

b. When Pew executes cross-national studies, it aims to complete all survey interviews in a three-to-six-week time period. Why is keeping the time period as short as possible important?

_____

_____

_____

_____

_____

_____

Exercise 10–9. Consider two different survey questions that measure support for the president:

Question 1: Do you *approve* or *disapprove* of the way Barack Obama is handling his job as president?

Question 2: How would you rate the job Barack Obama has been doing as president… do you *strongly approve, somewhat approve, somewhat disapprove,* or *strongly disapprove* of the job he's been doing?

In the first question, respondents are offered only two answer choices: "approve" and "disapprove." In the second question, respondents are offered four answer choices: "strongly approve," "somewhat approve," "somewhat disapprove," or "strongly disapprove." When Rasmussen, a polling organization, asked each of these questions to different but similar random samples of 800 likely voters in November 2009,[4] the results (with the answer choices for question 2 collapsed into "approve" and "disapprove" for comparison's sake) were:

Question 1: 50 percent "approve," 46 percent "disapprove," and 4 percent "don't know"

Question 2: 47 percent "approve," 52 percent "disapprove," and 1 percent "don't know"

a. Both random samples were similar, so why were the results different? In the space below, explain why you think the inclusion of the "somewhat" categories could have affected the results.

_____

_____

_____

_____

_____

b. How does this example help us better understand the importance of question wording?

_____

_____

_____

_____

Exercise 10-10.   Imagine that you are a student who is bored with an assignment on survey question writing. The assignment asks you to write a series of five questions you would ask of voters in a presidential election. To make things more interesting, you decide to write five questions that break all of the rules of question writing. In the space provided, write five bad survey questions and explain why they break the rules.

_____

_____

_____

_____

_____

_____

_____

_____

_____

_____

_____

_____

_____

_____

_____

_____

Exercise 10-11.   This item is a question for discussion and study.

Imagine that you have been granted immediate graduation from your school. Congratulations! You have also landed a very good job as an advisor to the president. The president is facing budget trouble and wants to know how voters will react to three policy proposals: a tax hike, a tax cut, or leaving tax rates unchanged. It is your job to decide upon a research design or strategy that would best suit the problem.

What you want to know is how public support for the president will change over time if taxes are cut, raised, or left at the status quo. Briefly answer the following questions: What type of research design would give you the best internal or external validity? How could you demonstrate that your results were reliable? What are the relative advantages of using a survey and an experiment? Would a small-_N_ design, such as a case study or a focus group, be useful? Would you want to use a cross-sectional design? A longitudinal design?

_____

_____

_____

_____

_____

_____

_____

_____

_____

_____

_____

NOTES

1. The American Presidency Project, "Political Party Platforms: Whig Party Platform of 1844," May 1, 1844, www.presidency.ucsb.edu/ws/index.php?pid=25852.

2. Pew Research Center, "Questionnaire Design and Translation," http://www.pewresearch.org/methodology/ international-survey-research/questionnaire-design-and- translation/.

3. You can read this passage and more about Pew's international survey efforts at http://www.pewresearch .org/methodology/international-survey-research/.

4. Mark Blumenthal, "Why Is Rasmussen So Different?" *Pollster.com*, December 1, 2009, www.pollster.com/blogs/ why_is_rasmussen_so_different.html.

11 MAKING SENSE OF DATA
First Steps

In chapter 11 of the text, we began the study of applied statistical analysis. The main goal of this study is to introduce some tools that can be used to summarize a batch of numbers and make inferences. These tools will help you in your coursework, in conducting your own research projects, and in interpreting statistics in the media. Furthermore, political science leads to quite a few interesting and exciting career opportunities, and many of these jobs require at least a rudimentary knowledge of quantitative research methods. Think, for example, of someone working for a nongovernmental organization like the World Health Organization. In all likelihood, her or his ability to interpret and apply statistics would be quite useful in analyzing health projects around the world. Or suppose you have an internship at a government agency. You may be of greater assistance to your employers if you can provide a modest amount of technical advice about reports they are receiving or information the agency supplies to the public. So there are lots of reasons for studying at least a few quantitative methods, no matter how far removed from the world of politics they seem to be.

Many students are initially put off by having to learn statistics, but our experience tells us that this aversion often results from unfamiliarity with the subject, not its inherent difficulty. So even if you are one who says, "I stink at math," at least attempt to keep an open mind because you may find that these concerns are misplaced.

Here are a few tips:

- **Keep up.** Unlike some subjects that may seem to lend themselves to cramming, statistics is best learned step by step; you should make sure you understand each concept reasonably well before moving on to the next one. And since the ideas are possibly daunting at first sight, it is easy to get lost if you try to learn everything all at once. This is, in short, one course where it pays to stay on top of the readings and assignments.

- **Learn by doing**. You cannot get into good physical shape by reading articles on conditioning. You have to work out regularly. In the same way and for essentially the same reasons, data analysis has to be learned actively. It is crucial that you perform your own analysis. Simply reading about how it is done will not give you the functional understanding that makes statistics so useful. The exercises in this workbook are designed to do just that: give you actual training in data analysis.

- **Keep substance over method**. Whenever possible think about the substantive context of a problem. You may be asked to calculate a mean or standard deviation, for example. But what is important is not the numbers per se (although they do have to be correct) but rather what they say about the problem at hand. For example, instead of just writing, "The average is ten," you should write, "The average is ten thousand dollars," to keep firmly in mind that you are working on a concrete issue and not an abstract algebra problem.

- **Be neat and orderly**. Yes, this advice sounds peevish. Yet we have found that a huge number of mistakes and misconceptions arise simply from disorderly note taking and hand calculations. It is always a good idea to have plenty of scrap paper handy and to work in a top-down fashion rather than jump all around the page putting intermediate calculations here and there in no logical order. It should be possible for you or anyone else to reconstruct your thought processes by following your calculations from beginning to end. That way errors and misunderstandings can be spotted and corrected.

- **A computer is only a tool.** Computers can compute answers to statistics problems and analyze data very quickly. Computers, however, cannot tell you what you need to solve a problem. When you begin analysis work on the computer, take a few moments to contemplate exactly what you need to complete a problem or an analysis. What do you need to find out? What procedure will give you the answers?

In these assignments we ask you to examine one variable at a time. The idea is to summarize a possibly large batch of numbers with a few indicators of a distribution's central tendency, dispersion, and shape. We have also appended a brief set of guidelines for preparing your own data for analysis.

Exercise 11-1.   In this first exercise, you should consider some of the basic terms that are key to understanding chapter 11. Some of these terms can sound too similar to differentiate or appear too complex to understand at first glance. For each pair of terms below, first define each term then explain the important differences between them.

a. Relative frequency and cumulative frequency

_____

_____

_____

b. Frequency and proportion

_____

_____

_____

c. Central tendency and dispersion

_____

_____

_____

d. Range and interquartile range

_____

_____

_____

e. Frequency distribution and normal distribution

_____

_____

_____

Exercise 11-2.   Measures of central tendency describe the typical value of a variable—the average, middle, or most frequently observed value. Below you will find variables that might arise in political science research, as well as a measure of central tendency. For each pairing explain why you think the selected measure would be appropriate or inappropriate. If you think it would be inappropriate, explain why you think a different measure would be a better choice. When answering the questions, make sure to consider levels of measurement and the possibilities of outliers or skewed data.

a. Variable: *type of political system*: indicates the political system in a country (democracy, dictatorship, monarchy, etc.)

Measure of central tendency: mean

_____

_____

b. Variable: *marital status*: indicates whether respondent is single, married, separated, divorced, widow(er)

Measure of central tendency: mode

_____

_____

c. Variable: *AIDS-related deaths:* number of AIDS-related deaths in a country in a year

Measure of central tendency: median

_____

_____

d. Variable: *annual household income*: dollar amount earned by each household in a year

Measure of central tendency: mean

_____

_____

e. Variable: *Environmental Performance Index*: a 0-to-100 score that measures 180 countries' performance across ten issue categories covering environmental health and ecosystem vitality

Measure of central tendency: median

_____

_____

f. Variable: *Internet connection speed*: indicates the average Internet connection speed in a country (1 = 0 to 4 Mbps; 2 = 4.1–8 Mbps; 3 = greater than 8 Mbps)

Measure of central tendency: mode

_____

_____

Exercise 11-3.   For this exercise you will use the sample data in table 11-1.

TABLE 11-1 ■ Hypothetical Number of Natural Disasters in Five Countries		
	Natural Disasters	Natural Disasters
i	Sample 1	Sample 2
1	5	1
2	5	4
3	5	5
4	5	5
5	5	10

a. Calculate the mean, median, and mode for each sample.

_____

b. Calculate the range and standard deviation for each sample.

_____

c. How does the data in table 11-1 help explain why it is important to calculate and consider measures of dispersion alongside measures of central tendency?

_____

_____

Exercise 11-4. In table 11-2 you will find estimated AIDS-related deaths in Central African countries in 2017 in the frequency column. Complete the table by calculating the proportion, percentage, and cumulative percentage.

TABLE 11-2 ■ Estimated AIDS-Related Deaths in Central Africa, 2017				
Country	Frequency	Proportion	Percentage	Cumulative Percentage
Angola	13,000			
Cameroon	24,000			
Central African Republic	5,200			
Chad	3,100			
Dem. Rep. of the Congo	17,000			
Rep. of Congo	4,900			
Equatorial Guinea	1,900			
Gabon	1,300			
Sao Tome and Principe	0			
	70,400			

Source: Data compiled from UN estimates, 2017, http://aidsinfo.unaids.org.

Exercise 11-5. This exercise is intended to help you familiarize yourself with the statistical package you will be using in class. The focus of this exercise is not on using or interpreting statistics but on introducing you to commonly used tools and commands that you will be using on a regular basis. You will be using the "States" data set available on the student Web site at https://edge.sagepub.com/johnson9e. On the Web site, you will find the file in multiple formats, including a comma-separated format, which can be used to create a file for just about any software package. You should use the package your instructor chooses.

The first step is to locate and save a copy of the "States" file. Good data practice includes making sure that your data is saved frequently so you do not lose your hard work. If you are working in a computer lab, it is wise to use a flash drive or cloud storage rather than saving your work on a lab computer where the file may be erased by another user. Saving your work frequently while working with data is a very good idea. I suggest that you get in the practice of saving multiple iterations of data files. For example, after working on a file for twenty minutes or so, or before making big changes to a data set, I will save a file as a new iteration. If working with the "States" file, I might call the first save "States1." Then, after working for a while, I would save a new copy called "States2," then "States3," and so on. By following this protocol, I will have saved a history of my work. If I should realize that I have made a mistake somewhere along the line, I can go back to the last save previous to the mistake without having to start all over.

Now that you have the "States" file open and saved, it is time to begin. Complete each step below. Please remember that while every software package has slightly different names for commands, the basic steps you are taking below are common to all software packages. You might just have to poke around a bit and find the correct command.

a. Visual inspection

Before beginning any project, it is wise to inspect the data so you understand what you have. The "States" data have one row for each of the fifty states and a column for each variable. Take a look at the kinds of variables that are available in the data set. You will see that there is a wide array of information in the file about the states.

b. Select cases.

The first step is to reduce the size of the data set. We want to work with only the nonsouthern states that gave Donald Trump greater than 45 percent of the presidential vote in 2016. Delete the southern states from the data using the *south* variable. Delete states that gave Trump less than or equal to 45 percent of the presidential vote in 2016 using the *Trump Vote Percentage* variable.

c. Sort cases.

Sort the states by population and list the five most populous states here, with the most populous state in space 1:

1. _____   2. _____   3. _____   4. _____   5. _____

Sort cases by religiosity and persons over sixty-five and list the five states that were most religious in order from highest percentage of persons over age sixty-five (space 1) to lowest (space 5) here:

(*Hint:* 3 is the most religious and 1 is the least on the variable *religiosity*)

1. _____   2. _____   3. _____   4. _____   5. _____

d. Create a new variable.

Create a new dichotomous variable that indicates whether a state had more than 65 percent turnout in the 2016 presidential election. A dichotomous variable is a variable with two categories. It is often advantageous to code a dichotomous variable with the values of 1 and 0, where 1 means that the characteristic measured by the variable is present and 0 means that the characteristic is absent. For this variable, which you will call *highturnout*, use a 1 when the characteristic is present (high turnout > 65 percent) and a 0 when the characteristic is absent (not high turnout < =65 percent).

e. Create a pie chart that demonstrates the proportion of high-turnout states to low-turnout states.

f. Label the pie chart to indicate > 65 percent and < =65 percent turnout. Give the pie chart a descriptive title.

g. Create a table that includes the mean vote percentage for Trump and Clinton in 2016 in the selected states.

h. Give the table a descriptive title.

i. Copy and paste your pie chart, table, and associated titles into a single document to turn in with this page.

Exercise 11-6. Using the hypothetical data in table 11-3, calculate the sample variance and sample standard deviation. Next, calculate the population variance and the population standard deviation using the same data. After completing your calculations, explain in plain English why the answers are different for the sample and population equations. How and why are the formulae different?

TABLE 11-3 ■ Political Events Attended	
Respondent Identification	Number of Political Events Attended in Last Year
1	4
2	3
3	0
4	1
5	7
6	3
7	1
8	0
9	5
10	1

Exercise 11-7. Use the data in table 11-4 to answer the following questions about central tendency and dispersion. You will need to think about which statistics best represent the data.

TABLE 11-4 ■ Military Spending 2017, Selected Countries	
Country	Military Spending[a]
United States	610
China	228
Saudi Arabia	69
Russia	66
India	64
France	58
UK	47
Japan	45
Germany	44
South Korea	39
Brazil	29
Italy	29

Source: Stockholm International Peace Research Institute, https://www.sipri.org/databases/milex.

[a] Military spending in billions, rounded to a whole number.

a.   What is the mean military spending?

b. What is the median military spending?

_____

c. What is the trimmed mean military spending? (Drop the minimum and maximum values.)

_____

d. Comment on the difference between the mean, the median, and the trimmed mean in this context. Which do you think is the best value to use to describe central tendency?

_____

_____

_____

e. What is the maximum value? _____ The minimum value? _____ The range? _____

_____

f. What is the first quartile (Q1)? _____ The third quartile (Q3)? _____ The interquartile range (IQR)? _____

g. Which measure of dispersion is the most appropriate choice for these data, the range or the interquartile range? Why?

Exercise 11-8. Table 11-5 reports the number of nuclear power plants in U.S. states.

TABLE 11-5 ■ Nuclear Power Plants in U.S. States	
State	**Nuclear Power Plants**
Connecticut	1
Florida	3
Illinois	6
Michigan	3
Mississippi	1
New Jersey	3
Ohio	2
Pennsylvania	5
South Carolina	4
Virginia	2

Source: Data are from NBC News, https://www.nbcnews.com/businessmain/10-states-run-nuclear-power-169050.

Compute the following descriptive statistics, treating these data as the *population* of all U.S. states with nuclear power plants:

a. Mean

b. Variance

c. Standard deviation

d. Interpret the mean and standard deviation in a single sentence that describes the nuclear power plant data.

Exercise 11-9. Table 11-6 reports the minimum wage in eight states.

TABLE 11-6 ■ State Minimum Wage as of January 1, 2019	
State	**Minimum Wage**
Alaska	9.89
Florida	8.46
Minnesota	9.86
Montana	8.50
New Jersey	8.85
Ohio	8.55
South Dakota	9.10
Vermont	10.78

Source: Data are from National Conference of State Legislatures, "2019 Minimum Wages by State," http://www.ncsl.org/research/labor-and-employment/state-minimum-wage-chart.aspx.

Compute the following descriptive statistics, treating these data as a *sample* of all states.

a. Mean

_____

b. Variance

_____

c. Standard deviation

_____

d. Interpret the mean and standard deviation in a single sentence that describes the minimum wage data.

_____

Exercise 11-10.   Figure 11-1 contains two distributions, A and B.

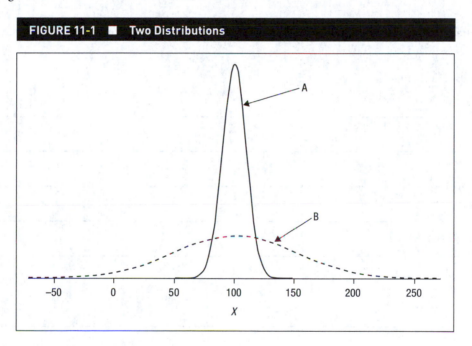

FIGURE 11-1 ■ Two Distributions

a. Which distribution has the greater variation? _____

b. Which distribution has the smaller standard deviation? _____

c. How do measures of central tendency for distributions A and B differ, if they differ at all?

_____

d. What are the mean and the median of distribution A? _____

e. What are the mean and the median of distribution B? _____

Exercise 11-11.   During the 2004 presidential campaign, there was a lot of discussion about who benefited from the tax cuts initiated and signed into law by the George W. Bush administration. Senator John Kerry said, "George Bush's only economic plan is lavish tax breaks for those at the top." President Bush asserted proudly, "I have twice led the United States Congress to pass historic tax relief for the American people." Part of the argument turned on dollar amounts received by different groups. A White House news release claimed, "Under the President's proposal to speed up tax relief, 92 million taxpayers would receive, on average, a tax cut of $1,083 in 2003."[1] Yet one of the president's critics wrote, "The average working family would get about $289."[2] Assuming both sides are telling the truth, how do you suppose they could reach such different conclusions? You will not be able to provide a definitive answer, but your knowledge of summary statistics should give you a good idea.

_____

_____

_____

_____

_____

_____

Exercise 11-12. Define as clearly as possible the following statistics. Try to explain each term in plain language.

a. The sample standard deviation

_____

_____

_____

_____

_____

b. The median

_____

_____

_____

_____

_____

c. The mode

_____

_____

_____

d. The trimmed mean

_____

_____

_____

_____

_____

e. The interquartile range

_____

_____

_____

_____

_____

Exercise 11-13. Internet access varies widely across the world. Some countries have near universal Internet access while others have very low rates of access. In this exercise you will attempt to create a box plot that summarizes and explores Internet access in South America in 2018 using data from table 11-7.

TABLE 11-7 ■ Percent of Population with Internet Access in South American Countries, 2018			
Country	**Internet Access**	**Sorted Country**	**Internet Access**
Argentina	93		
Bolivia	68		
Brazil	71		
Chile	78		
Colombia	63		
Ecuador	80		
Falkland Islands	99		
French Guiana	41		
Guyana	51		
Paraguay	90		
Peru	68		
Suriname	60		
Uruguay	88		
Venezuela	53		

Source: Data are from Internet World Stats, https://www.internetworldstats.com/stats5.htm#me.

Follow the steps below to create your box plot.

1. Sort the countries by Internet access from lowest percentage to highest percentage in the empty columns in table 11-7, with the country with the lowest percentage of access at the top of the column and the country with the highest percentage of access at the bottom of the column.

2. Find the maximum and minimum, the first and third quartiles, the interquartile range (IQR), and the median.

   Maximum: _____ Minimum: _____ First quartile: _____ Third quartile: _____

   Interquartile range: _____ Median: _____

3. Draw a horizontal line to indicate the scale of the variable. Mark off intervals of the variable. Be sure to fully label the scale.

4. Above the line, say about half an inch or so, draw a small vertical line to indicate the median. It should correspond to the appropriate value on the scale.

5. Next, draw short vertical lines of the same size above the scale to indicate Q1 and Q3.

6. Sketch a rectangle with the two quartiles (Q1 and Q3) at the ends. The median will be in the box somewhere. The height of the rectangle does not matter.

7. Draw a vertical line at the minimum for the lower whisker. Call this quantity "LW" for short.

8. Draw a line from the first quartile (Q1) to the point LW.

9. Do the same for the upper whisker. This time, however, you will use the maximum of the variable. Call the result "UW."

10. Draw a line from the third quartile (Q3) to the point UW.

11. Give the graph a title and properly label the x-axis.

Title: _____

APPENDIX TO CHAPTER 11

Preparing Data for Analysis

You may at some point be asked to collect data on your own. The textbook and the workbook provide examples of how the information can be organized for analysis by hand or computer. Here are a few specific tips that might speed up the process and help you avoid common mistakes.

Think of this step as more than just organizing and cleaning the data so that they can be easily analyzed by hand or (more likely) computer—it has theoretical importance as well. Among other tasks, this process requires checking for and correcting errors; looking for inconsistencies (for example, Canada coded as a Southeast Asian country); recoding or changing recorded information to make it more analytically tractable; combing or separating categories of nominal variables; and determining what are to be considered valid responses. These efforts are often invisible because research organizations (such as the one that conducts the National Election Studies) do much of the work before releasing the information to others.

- **Recording numbers.** Most computer programs insist that you enter numbers *without commas*. So, for example, 5,000 would be typed 5000. Moreover, *do not* use symbols such as the dollar ($) or percent (%) signs.

- **Plus and minus signs.** If the original data contain negative values, they have to be entered with a minus sign. Positive values are always entered *without* a plus sign.

- **Precision.** We use at most two decimal places, mainly for ease of calculation. Precision can be a tricky problem in statistical analysis. On one hand, in long, involved calculations, so-called round-off errors (the rounding of decimal numbers during intermediate steps) can rapidly accumulate and lead to results that differ from those based on exact numbers. On the other hand, when you present data tables to others, one or two decimal places are usually sufficient.

- **Labels versus names.** To facilitate computer analysis, each variable has a short label or tag. Most computer programs require relatively brief names or abbreviations, like the ones used here, but they can often handle separately entered longer descriptive labels. Note, however, that if a data matrix is to be published, every effort should be made to assign intelligible names to the variables. Otherwise, readers can easily lose the meanings of the tags.

- **Category combinations.** Sometimes you have to combine categories to achieve an optimal number of cases. For example, we might assign New Zealand to Asia and Morocco and Egypt to the Middle East to avoid having categories with just one or two observations. The key is to make the assignments as explicit as possible so that others can understand and, if need be, challenge or modify them.

- **Recoding.** It may or may not be necessary, depending on software, to recode text to numeric values. If we were using a variable that captured the level of development, this variable could be coded in more than one way. *Status*, for instance, could be simply reported as "developed" or "developing," or we could choose numeric codes 1 and 5, respectively, to stand for the substantive categories. The designation is arbitrary; we could use 1 and 2 or 50 and 500 or any other two numbers. Since development status is a nominal variable, the numbers do not have an intrinsic quantitative meaning. But, surprisingly perhaps, it is legitimate to make use of these arbitrary numbers in some statistical procedures by recoding them as dichotomous variables. We show how in chapter 14 of the textbook.

- **Missing data.** What do you do when data for a particular observation are not available because they were not collected or reported? This is the missing data problem. Imagine that a respondent did not answer one question on a survey form. Despite this, there is information for the remaining questions. When it is entered into a data set, we must indicate the missing information with an indicator—often 999 or some other repeating number, or a character, such as a single period. When our computer program encounters this symbol, it excludes the case for a particular procedure involving that variable and continues with its work. The result would be based on one fewer case. Do the respondents with and without reported values differ in any systematic ways? It is hard to tell, which explains why a lot of thought has to go into collecting and preparing data for analysis. Each of these seemingly trivial matters can have significant implications.[3] A rule of thumb is that if 20 percent or more of your cases have missing values for a variable, you might consider dropping it or finding one that has more complete information.

- **Error and consistency checking.** Always check for errors and inconsistencies. In many instances preliminary descriptive and exploratory analyses will alert you to the possibility of errors in the data. But this is not always the case, so if you are collecting data by hand, check and recheck the numbers.

- **Weights.** When certain sampling designs are used to collect the data, it may be necessary to adjust the numbers to reflect over- or underrepresentation of certain groups. If you download data from the Internet, always check. (Most, but alas not all, software allows you to identify a weighted variable and will adjust the data for you.) In this book, however, weighting is never a problem.

NOTES

1. The White House, "Fact Sheet: President Bush Taking Action to Strengthen America's Economy," January 2003, http://georgewbush-whitehouse.archives.gov/news/releases/2003/01/20030107.html.

2. Kathryn Casa, "The Elephant in the Room," *CounterPunch*, http://www.counterpunch.org/casa01292003.html.

3. An enormous amount of thought has gone into the problem of missing data. For a review of a few statistical solutions, see Joseph L. Schafer and John W. Graham, "Missing Data: Our View of the State of the Art," *Psychological Methods* 7 (2002): 147–77.

12 TESTING RELATIONSHIPS

Chapter 12 of the textbook expanded on the introduction to statistics found in chapter 11, moving from basic statistical concepts like central tendency and dispersion to more complex concepts like hypothesis testing and confidence intervals. While chapter 11 explained how statistics can be used to explore data, chapter 12 focused on making inferences using statistics. In this chapter in the workbook, you will be asked to use your new statistical skills to analyze data to answer questions.

Exercise 12-1. Terms in this chapter can be easily confused with each other. It is important that you understand each term and how it fits into the broader context of testing relationships. Below you will find pairs of statistical terms. Provide a definition of each term and explain the difference between the terms.

a. Type I error and type II error

_____

_____

_____

b. Confidence level and confidence interval

_____

_____

_____

c. t score and t-test

_____

_____

_____

d. t score and z score

_____

_____

_____

Exercise 12-2. Have you considered why we can use sample statistics for any variable? How can we use inferential statistics with a ratio-level variable such as income, an ordinal variable measuring education, or a dichotomous variable measuring gender? The answer is that each variable is normally distributed in its sampling distribution. For this exercise you will explore the sampling distribution for a variable that is binomial: a coin flip. It is binomial because it has only two categories, heads and tails. While you cannot ever observe a sampling distribution because it is created with an infinite number of samples—which we can of course never complete—you can begin to see how a sampling distribution might look. For this exercise you will need a coin. Below you will record the results of ten series of coin flips, with ten flips in each series. You will flip the coin ten times and record the total number of heads you observe in the space marked Series 1. You will then proceed to flip the coin ten more times and record your observations for Series 2, and so on. Once you have recorded all your observations, use a histogram (review chapter 11) to visually display the results from the ten series (the number of heads observed in each series) in the space to the right. How does tossing coins demonstrate the concept of the sampling distribution?

Example: Seven heads (I flipped my coin ten times and counted seven heads, so I wrote seven in the blank.)

Series 1: _____ heads

Series 2: _____ heads

Series 3: _____ heads

Series 4: _____ heads

Series 5: _____ heads

Series 6: _____ heads

Series 7: _____ heads

Series 8: _____ heads

Series 9: _____ heads

Series 10: _____ heads

Exercise 12-3. Using the data in table 12-1, compute a z score to determine the percentage chance of observing a country with 6 percent unemployment or more. Show your work.

a. Draw the normal distribution here. Label information as you go to keep track of everything. Include the X and Z scales.

b. Calculate the mean and population standard deviation and record your answer on the line below.

_____

c. Calculate the z score and record your answer on the line below.

_____

d. What is the probability associated with your calculated z score?

_____

e. What is the percentage chance of observing a country with 6 percent unemployment or more?

_____

TABLE 12-1 ■ Unemployment Percentage	
	Unemployment (%)
Belgium	7
France	10
Ireland	6
Luxembourg	6
Monaco	2
Netherlands	5
United Kingdom	4

Source: Central Intelligence Agency, *The World Factbook*, https://www.cia.gov/library/publications/the-world-factbook/rankorder/2129rank.html.

Exercise 12-4.   Using the data in table 12-2, calculate a sample confidence interval for life expectancy in Western Europe, treating the data as sample data. For this confidence interval, use a 95 percent confidence level. Show your work.

a. What is the mean and sample standard deviation?

b. Record the confidence limit.

c. What is the standard error of the mean?

d. What is the sample confidence interval? (*Hint:* Make sure to include the alpha level for proper interpretation!)

TABLE 12-2 ■ Life Expectancy in Western European Countries	
	Life Expectancy
Belgium	81
France	82
Ireland	81
Luxembourg	82
Monaco	89
Netherlands	81
United Kingdom	81

Source: Central Intelligence Agency, *The World Factbook*, https://www.cia.gov/library/publications/the-world-factbook/rankorder/2102rank.html.

Exercise 12-5.   We can use a confidence interval to determine the interval in which we expect to find the population mean, given a certain level of confidence. The interval we find using this statistic varies based on the values of the standard deviation, the sample size, and the confidence level. In the following problems, you will manipulate the values used in a *population confidence interval* to learn how changes in these values affect the size of the confidence interval. Show your work.

Population Confidence Interval

Calculate the population confidence interval with a sample mean of 5, a sample size of 500, a confidence level of 95 percent, and a population standard deviation of 2.

_____

_____

_____

_____

Change in Standard Deviation

In the first step, you calculated the population confidence interval with a mean of 5, a sample size of 500, a confidence level of 95 percent, and a standard deviation of 2. In this step you are going to analyze the effect of changing the size of the standard deviation. This time, calculate the population confidence interval with a mean of 5, a sample size of 500, a confidence level of 95 percent, and a standard deviation of 4. How does a larger standard deviation affect the calculation of a confidence interval? Why is this so?

_____

_____

_____

_____

_____

Change in Sample Size

In the first step, you calculated the population confidence interval with a mean of 5, a sample size of 500, a confidence level of 95 percent, and a standard deviation of 2. This time, calculate the population confidence interval with a mean of 5, a sample size of 1,000, a confidence level of 95 percent, and a standard deviation of 2. How does a larger sample size affect the calculation of a confidence interval? Why is this so?

_____

_____

_____

_____

Change in Confidence Level

In the first step, you calculated the population confidence interval with a mean of 5, a sample size of 500, a confidence level of 95 percent, and a standard deviation of 2. Now calculate the population confidence interval with a mean of 5, a sample size of 500, a confidence level of 90 percent, and a standard deviation of 2. How does a lower confidence level affect the calculation of a confidence interval? Why is this so?

_____

_____

_____

_____

_____

Exercise 12-6.   For this exercise you should refer to the definition and explanation of type I and type II errors in chapter 12 in the textbook, then think about the following hypothetical research project. Imagine that the U.S. government is interested in increasing election turnout and has announced a $100 million grant to fund a program to increase voter turnout. As a brilliant political science student, you feel certain that offering civics classes to voting-eligible adults would improve turnout rates. You think that voters would surely turn out at a higher rate if they only knew how vital participation is to democracy. To support your application for the $100 million, you use your new methodological skills to test the hypothesis that likelihood of voting increases after taking a civics class.

In the space provided below, explain the consequences of making a type I error and a type II error when testing your hypothesis about the relationship between civics classes and the likelihood of voting.

_____

_____

_____

_____

_____

_____

Exercise 12-7.   For this exercise you will need to consult appendices A and B in the text. For each of the following questions, use the appropriate appendix to find the answer.

a.   Find the probability associated with a z score of 1.20.

_____

b.   Find the probability associated with a z score of 2.25.

_____

c. Find the *z* score associated with a probability of .2912.

_____

d. Find the *z* score associated with a probability of .0062.

_____

e. Find a *t* score using a two-tailed test, an alpha level of .05, and ten degrees of freedom.

_____

f. Find a *t* score using a one-tailed test, an alpha level of .01, and fifteen degrees of freedom.

_____

g. Why is the largest probability listed in appendix A .5000?

_____

_____

h. Why do the probabilities in appendix A get smaller as the *z* scores get larger?

_____

_____

i. Why are *t* scores larger with fewer degrees of freedom and smaller with more degrees of freedom?

_____

_____

j. (1) Find the probability associated with a *z* score of 1.96. (2) Find *t* scores using a two-tailed test, a .05 alpha level, and an infinite degree of freedom. What is the important relationship between the first and second probabilities you just found?

_____

_____

_____

_____

Exercise 12-8.   Many of the statistics in chapter 12 rely on the concept of statistical significance. To assert statistical significance, one can compare a test or observed value to a critical value from a distribution, such as the normal distribution or student's *t* distribution. In appendix B of the textbook, you will find a table containing critical values from the *t* distribution. For each set of circumstances in table 12-3, indicate whether the observed value is sufficient to assert statistical significance. (*Hint:* Remember that in order to be statistically significant, the absolute value of the observed *t* value should be greater than the *t*-critical value).

TABLE 12-3 ■ Finding Statistical Significance Using the *t*-Distribution

Number of Tails in Test	Confidence Level	Degrees of Freedom	*t*-Observed	*t*-Critical	Statistically Significant
Two	99%	21	2.95	2.831	yes
Two	95%	25	−3.10		
Two	95%	15	−2.12		
Two	90%	10	1.94		
Two	90%	18	1.57		
One	99%	12	−2.46		
One	99%	23	2.38		
One	98.5%	40	−2.30		
One	95%	28	1.89		
One	95%	16	1.68		

Exercise 12-9.   The next set of questions is designed to help you get used to translating a political claim into a statistical hypothesis that can be tested.

According to the U.S. Census Bureau, "The nation's public school districts spent an average of $8,701 per student on elementary and secondary education in fiscal year 2005, up 5 percent from the previous year."[1] A staff member for a candidate for governor has conducted a random sample of fifteen school districts and found that the mean spending level is only $8,000 per pupil. The candidate is using this finding to support his charge that the incumbent is weak on education. The newspaper you work for wants to know whether the difference between the population mean ($8,701) and the sample mean ($8,000) suggests that on the whole your state spends less on education than the rest of the country or if the results are likely due to sampling error.

a. Write a null hypothesis for this problem.

b. Write an alternative hypothesis. (*Hint:* Think carefully about the context. The candidate's argument is that the state spends less than the rest of the country.)

c. What statistical test would you use to evaluate the null hypothesis? Why?

d. What would be the appropriate sampling distribution? Why?

Exercise 12-10.   There are many different ways to test a hypothesis. In chapter 12 in the textbook, we explained how to use a two-sided and a one-sided *t*-test. In the space following, please explain the circumstances under which you would use a one-sided *t*-test and a two-sided *t*-test. Next, use the hypothetical sample data in table 12-4 to perform a sample *t*-test testing the sample mean against a test value of 1. Use the 95 percent confidence level and calculate the critical *t* value using both a one-sided and two-sided test. How do these calculations illustrate the difference between the two tests?

_____

_____

_____

_____

_____

_____

TABLE 12-4 ■ Demonstration Data for *t*-Tests	
i	*x*
1	4
2	3
3	6
4	0
5	2
6	3

Exercise 12-11.   The data in table 12-5 indicate the percentage of exports Botswana sends to each of its five largest trading partners. Imagine that the mean for the population, all countries, is 18 percent of exports to major trading partners. Calculate a difference of means *t*-test to test the null hypothesis that Botswana's export percentage to its largest trading partners is no different from the population mean of 18 percent. Use the 95 percent confidence level. Show your work.

a.   What is the observed *t* score?

_____

b.   What is the *t*-critical value (using a two-tailed test because the direction of the hypothesis is not specified)?

_____

c.   Do you accept or reject the null hypothesis and why?

_____

_____

_____

TABLE 12-5 ■ Percentage of Exports from Botswana to Largest Trading Partners, 2017	
Botswana's Largest Trading Partners	**Percentage of Botswana's Exports**
Belgium	22
India	20
United Arab Emirates	17
South Africa	9
Singapore	8

Source: The World Bank, World Integrated Trade Solution, https://wits.worldbank.org/CountrySnapshot/en/BWA/textview.

Exercise 12-12.   Imagine that you have access to sample data from the U.S. State Department about the amount of money different nations spend on educational programs designed to foster goodwill with citizens from other countries. While you would prefer full access to the data, the State Department agrees to tell you only the population mean and to provide you with a sample of the population data. You reluctantly agree, pending verification that the sample data is representative of the population data. The population mean is $13.4 million. The hypothetical sample data to which you have access is listed in table 12-6. Use a *t*-test to determine whether the data to which you have access is representative of the population data by testing the mean of your data against the population mean provided by the State Department. You should use a two-tailed test and a 95 percent confidence level. Explain how a *t*-test could help you decide whether using the sample data is sufficient. Show your work.

TABLE 12-6 ■ Millions of Dollars Spent Fostering Goodwill	
Country	**Millions of Dollars**
Brazil	8
Canada	16
Denmark	11
Ghana	5
Kuwait	6
India	9
Malaysia	1
South Africa	8
South Korea	10
United Kingdom	18

_____

_____

Exercise 12-13.   For this exercise you will use a difference of means test to test the hypothesis that older citizens hold the Supreme Court in higher regard than do younger citizens. The data include two random samples drawn independently.[2] Sample 1 includes thirty citizens who are forty years of age or older and has a sample mean of 87 and a sample standard deviation of 4. Sample 2 includes twenty-five citizens under age forty and has a sample mean of 85 and a sample standard deviation of 3. Choose a confidence level with which you are comfortable and explain why you chose that level. Then decide if you accept the hypothesis. (*Hint:* Use the formula for calculating a *t*-test with independent samples.) Show your work.

_____

_____

_____

_____

_____

_____

Exercise 12-14.   The calculations for difference of means *t*- and *z*-tests include several parts, including the difference of the means, the standard deviation, and the sample size. Suppose that another student in the class does not understand how the difference of the means, the standard deviation, or the sample size affects the *t* and *z* values when using a *t*-test or a *z*-test. In the spaces provided, please explain how changes in each item affect the *t* and *z* values and the likelihood of finding statistical significance.

a.   A larger standard deviation

_____

_____

_____

b.   A larger sample size

_____

_____

_____

c.   A larger difference of the means

_____

_____

_____

d. What is the standard error of the mean? What does it tell us about our data, and why is it important in testing hypotheses?

_____

_____

_____

_____

_____

_____

Exercise 12-15. In chapter 12 in the textbook, we explain how you can use a confidence interval to test a hypothesis. Imagine that you are working on a research project on the representation of women in national legislatures. You have data on the percentage of women in national legislatures in a sample of African countries. Using the data in table 12-7, calculate a sample confidence interval and use the confidence interval to test the following hypothesis: *Female membership in African legislatures is not different from the world mean of 23 percent.* Decide whether you should accept or reject your hypothesis and explain why you would do so. Use a .05 alpha level and a two-tailed test. Show your work.

TABLE 12-7 ■ Seats Held by Women in Selected National Legislatures, 2018	
Country	**Women in National Legislature (Percentage)**
Cameroon	31
Chad	13
Gambia	10
Ghana	13
Namibia	46
Rwanda	61
Uganda	34

Source: Inter-Parliamentary Union, "Women in National Parliaments," June 1, 2018, http://archive.ipu.org/wmn-e/arc/classif010618.htm.

_____

_____

_____

_____

_____

Exercise 12-16. It is time to see how statistics software tests a hypothesis. Consider an estimate of life expectancy. A classmate has estimated that life expectancy worldwide is probably about seventy-two years. You will use a *t*-test to determine if there is a statistical difference between the classmate's estimated life expectancy and the real life expectancy.

Null hypothesis H_0: life expectancy = 71

Alternative hypothesis H_A: life expectancy ≠ 71

For this exercise you will be using the "Human Development Index" data set available on the student Web site at https://edge.sagepub.com/johnson9e. The data were collected by the United Nations and used to create an index of human development in each country based on life expectancy, income, and educational attainment. Open the file and select the *Life Expectancy* variable.

a. You will use 71 as the test value in your hypothesis test. In other words, you will enter 71 in the statistical package *t*-test and test 71 against the mean of the *Life Expectancy* variable. Report your observed *t* score on the line below. Then explain whether there is a statistically significant difference between the values and how you came to that decision. Use a 95 percent confidence level (two-tailed test).

_____

_____

_____

Exercise 12-17.   In this exercise you will be using a software package in testing a hypothesis.

Imagine that during a lecture on voting behavior, your professor claimed that despite the widespread use of social media, only 20 percent of people use social media to discuss politics. As a student of data analysis, you have decided to test this claim. Using the "Social Vote" data set, test the following hypotheses using the *t*-test for proportions method:

Null hypothesis H_0: proportion of those who share political information on social media = .2

Alternative hypothesis H_A: proportion of those who share political information on social media ≠ .2

You will test the hypothesis using the *Shared Opinion* variable in the "Social Vote" data set available on the Web site at https://edge.sagepub.com/johnson9e. This data set was collected by the Pew Research Center and includes data about how people used social media during the 2012 presidential election. The *Shared Opinion* variable includes respondents' answers to the following question: "Have you let other people know who you voted for, or who you plan to vote for, in this year's election by posting that information on a social networking site such as Facebook or Twitter?"

a. Use a software package to open the "Social Vote" data file and use the package to find the proportion of 1s to 0s and the standard deviation for the *Shared Opinion* variable. Treat all other values as missing or delete the cases with other values. Report the answers here:

_____

b. Calculate a *t* score using a test of a proportion as outlined in the text. Use the proportion and standard deviation you calculated in part a using a 95 percent confidence level and a two-tailed test.

_____

c. Do you accept the professor's statement as true? Why or why not?

_____

_____

_____

Exercise 12-18.   In this exercise you will use software to find a sample confidence interval. Open the "Human Development Index" file and take a look at the *Human Development Index (HDI)* variable. This variable measures human development in each of the countries in the data set. The data were collected by the United Nations and used to create an index of human development in each country based on life expectancy, income, and educational attainment. For this problem we want to compute a 95 percent confidence interval (two-tailed test) and treat the data as if it were sample data. Compute the 95 percent confidence interval and then answer the questions below.

a. What are the mean and the standard deviation for the *Human Development Index (HDI)* variable?

_____

b. What is the value of the standard error of the mean in the confidence interval?

_____

c. What is the confidence interval?

_____

NOTES

1. U.S. Census Bureau, "Public Education Finances," Census Project Update, http://www.census.gov/mp/www/cpu/factoftheday/010196.html.

2. Like the example in the text, you should assume the variances are equal.

13 ANALYZING RELATIONSHIPS FOR CATEGORICAL DATA

Chapters 13 and 14 in the textbook discussed the analysis of relationships between variables. Two variables are statistically related when values of the observations for one variable are associated with values of the observations for the other. This workbook chapter and the one that follows give you a chance to investigate several aspects of relationships between two or more variables, including strength, direction or shape, and statistical significance.

We mention throughout the textbook that plenty of career opportunities exist for political scientists who have a reasonable understanding of quantitative methods. So if you know a little about cross-tabulations, regression analysis, and statistical inference, you may find jobs waiting for you in governmental and nongovernmental organizations, or in firms or industries that have little to do with political science. Experience tells us that employers look for well-trained social scientists who can clearly, succinctly, and forcefully explain numerical procedures and results to people who do not have much knowledge of these topics. This ability becomes particularly valuable when someone asks, "Is this an important finding, one I should pay attention to, or can I ignore it?" Hence, we encourage you to think carefully about the answers to the questions posed here and in other chapters.

Here we offer some advice for translating statistical results into accessible language:

- **Before responding to the question (or submitting a report to your boss), consider what is being asked**. In the real world, people want answers expressed in real-world terms. You have been told that a regression coefficient, for example, can be interpreted as the slope of a line or as indicating how much Y changes for each unit increase or decrease in X. An r measures goodness of fit. But for many people, explanations expressed in those terms might as well be gibberish. It is essential, then, that you make sense of statistical terms by placing them in a specific substantive context. Regression and correlation coefficients indicate how and how strongly one thing is related to another. That's the importance of such coefficients. So make sure that you talk about variables, not equations or Greek letters or abstract symbols. For example, write "Income is related to attitudes on taxation," not "X is related to Y."

- **Go even further to explain the nature of interconnections**. Yes, income is correlated with opinions. But how? You might add, "The wealthier people are, the more they favor cutting taxes, but even the lower and middle classes want some degree of tax relief." This statement is much more informative to a nonstatistician than the statement "There's a positive correlation."

- **We have suggested numerous times that the definitions of variables determine how we interpret the phenomena under consideration.** People want to know if there is a meaningful difference between A and B, or they want to understand how strongly X and Y are connected. Numbers alone won't do the job. Only the names and meanings of the variables will. So don't write something like, "There is a difference of ten (or a difference of ten units)." The difference is in what units? Dollars? Years? Pounds? Percentages?

- **In this same vein, the measurement scales of variables are critically important.** They should be one of the first things you look for and understand. In some cases the meaning of the categories or the intervals will be obvious or intuitive, as in "years of formal schooling." In other instances a scale may present more subtle explanatory difficulties. Take income, a variable we discuss several times in the text. In many cases the scale is just "dollars," so "$1,000" has a clear meaning. In other instances a variable may be measured in thousands, millions, or even billions of dollars. (That is, "$10" may stand for "$10 million.") It is important that you know exactly which scale is being used. After all, a change of ten means one thing when we are talking about simple dollars and quite another when the scale is millions or billions. And complicating matters even further, social scientists often measure variables on abstract or artificial scales. ("Where would you place yourself on this 10-point thermometer of feelings about the president?") If one person's score is 7 and another's is 5, the scores differ. But how important in the world of politics is this difference? As we emphasize below, it is only possible to give a reasoned judgment; there will seldom be a clearly right or wrong answer.

- **You can help yourself by keeping track of measures of central tendency and variability**. If most respondents in a study have values near the mean or median, then one person whose score is two standard deviations away may be unusual and warrant further investigation. Was the individual's score measured correctly? Is he or she an "extremist?" The two interpretations, which have vastly different substantive implications, can be adjudicated only with thought and perhaps further research.

- **Do not let one or two measures (for example, chi-square or ρ) do all your interpretative work.** Instead, try to examine the data as a whole. If you have a contingency table, look for patterns of association within the table's body. Compare different categories of the response patterns. For example, individuals at the high and low ends of a scale often differ greatly in their attitudes. Those in the middle may be more homogeneous. Or response patterns may differ as you move from one end of the table to the other. Whatever the case, it is important to examine data, such as that found in a table, from several angles. Similarly, variables having quantitative (ratio and interval) scales should be plotted as they are in the text. (Graphing software is so widely available that this shouldn't be a chore.) From such graphics you can determine the form of relationships and their strength and locate "outlying" observations, among other things.

- **As we noted, assessing importance is one of the hardest tasks facing data analysts.** This problem has both statistical and substantive aspects, and both have to be considered simultaneously. Terms such as *statistical significance* and *explained variation* pertain to observed data, not to people's feelings and behavior. Therefore, finding that a chi-square is statistically significant may or may not be important. By the same token, the fact that income "explains 60 percent of the variation in political ideology" doesn't necessarily mean we know much about why people are liberals, moderates, or conservatives. Data analysis helps us understand, but it does not replace hard thought about the substance of a topic.

Exercise 13-1. Below you will find a number of statistics for use with categorical variables. You will notice that each statistic has a name based on a Greek letter. In order to reinforce the name and purpose of each statistic, match the statistic with its purpose by writing the correct number in the space after each statistic. The Greek letter that represents the statistic is in parentheses.

a. Chi square (χ^2)   _____

b. Eta-squared (η^2)   _____

c. Gamma (γ)   _____

d. Lambda (λ)   _____

e. Tau-b (τ_b)   _____

f. Phi (Φ)   _____

1. A measure of association between ordinal-level variables

2. An association measure that adjusts an observed chi-square statistic by the sample size

3. Measure of association between ordinal-level variables

4. A statistic used to test whether a relationship is statistically significant in a cross-tabulation table

5. A measure of association used with the analysis of variance that indicates what proportion of the variance in the dependent variable is explained by the variance in the independent variable

6. A measure of association between one nominal- or ordinal-level variable and one nominal-level variable

Exercise 13-2. Chapter 13 in the textbook discussed cross-tabulation as it relates to the analysis of two variables. Answer each of the following questions about why and how we might use a cross-tabulation for analysis.

a. Cross-tabulations are for categorical data. What are categorical data? How would you define a categorical variable?

_____

_____

b. Why would it be difficult—if not impossible—to use a cross-tabulation to examine two variables that capture continuous data rather than categorical data?

_____

_____

c. When the categories of the independent variable are arrayed across the *top* of a cross-tabulation table—that is, they are the column labels—why is it essential that the column percentages equal 100?

_____

_____

d. For what purpose would you use gamma in analyzing data in a cross-tabulation?

_____

_____

e. How would you interpret a gamma value of 1? How would you interpret a gamma value of -1?

_____

_____

f. How much magnitude (the distance from 0) would you want to see in gamma before concluding that there is a strong relationship between the variables?

_____

_____

Exercise 13-3. Statisticians frequently use graphs to visualize relationships. Look at figure 13-1. It displays what we have labeled a strong "negative linear correlation" between *Y* and *X*.

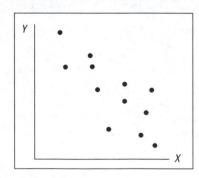

FIGURE 13-1 ■ Example of Negative Linear Correlation

a. Describe the type and (approximate) strength of the four relationships shown in figure 13-2.

_____

_____

FIGURE 13-2   ■   Examples of Correlations

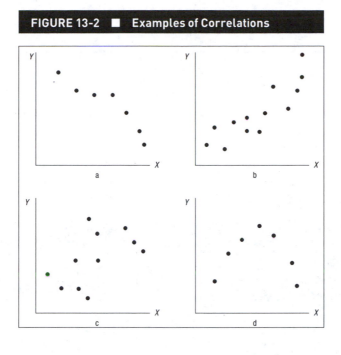

_____

_____

_____

_____

_____

_____

Exercise 13-4. Using the data in table 13-1, create a contingency table to examine the relationship between ethnicity and political participation, as measured by voting. Make sure that you include the appropriate percentages as well as the frequencies.

TABLE 13-1   ■   Legality of Home Schooling in European Countries

Countries	Homeschooling	N
Eastern European	Legal	10
Eastern European	Illegal	17
Non-Eastern European	Legal	10
Non-Eastern European	Illegal	10

Source: Nationmaster.com, https://www.nationmaster.com/country-info/stats/Education/Homeschooling-legal-status.

a. Attach your table.

b. In your opinion, does a relationship exist between Eastern European countries and homeschooling? Briefly explain your answer.

_____

_____

_____

_____

_____

_____

_____

Exercise 13-5. Table 13-2 is a contingency table from a computer program that shows the relationship between region and the political parties of ninety-nine U.S. senators. (One independent senator is not included.)

TABLE 13-2 ■ Cross-Tabulation of Senators' Party Identification and Region					
	Region				
Party Identification	1	2	3	4	Total
1. Democrat	16	9	14	10	49
% within region	69.6%	37.5%	53.8%	38.5%	49.5%
2. Republican	7	15	12	16	50
% within region	30.4%	62.5%	46.2%	61.5%	50.5%
Total	23	24	26	26	99
% within region	100.0%	100.0%	100.0%	100.0%	100.0%

Source: Computer-generated table.

a. Do the data indicate that Democratic and Republican senators tend to come from different regions of the country?

_____

_____

b. If you did not know which region a senator was from, what would be your best guess of his or her party affiliation?

_____

_____

c. What would be an appropriate measure of association? Why?

_____

_____

_____

d. Calculate the measure that you identified in part c.

_____

_____

Exercise 13-6.   Examine the data presented in table 13-3.

TABLE 13-3 ■ Cross-Tabulation of Prayer by Political Ideology

| PRAY: How often does respondent pray? | Political Orientation | | | Total |
	1 Liberal	2 Moderate	3 Conservative	
1. Several times a day	33	71	91	195
	18.0%	23.9%	41.7%	27.9%
2. Once a day	53	86	64	203
	29.0%	29.0%	29.4%	29.1%
3. Several times a week	22	48	25	95
	12.0%	16.2%	11.5%	13.6%
4. Once a week	17	18	14	49
	9.3%	6.1%	6.4%	7.0%
5. Less than once a week	55	72	23	150
	30.1%	24.2%	10.6%	21.5%
6. Never	3	2	1	6
	1.6%	.7%	.5%	.9%
Total	183	297	218	698
	100.0%	100.0%	100.0%	100.0%

Source: Computer-generated table.

a.   Which is the independent variable? Which is the dependent variable? Describe the relationship between the variables.

_____

_____

_____

_____

_____

_____

b.   The gamma value for the data in the table is −.288. What does gamma tell you about the relationship between political orientation and frequency of praying? Why does gamma have a negative sign?

_____

_____

_____

_____

_____

_____

Exercise 13-7.   In this exercise you will analyze data using a chi-square test. Use the hypothetical data in table 13-4 to assess whether the variables are statistically independent. Remember that the chi-square statistic is not a very good indicator of the strength of an association. If this were a full analysis of the data, you might measure strength through an analysis of percentages. Here we are simply using chi-square to test for statistical significance. Use a one-tailed test and $\alpha = .05$.

TABLE 13-4 ■ Relationship between X and Y Based on Sample of 200			
		Variable X	
Variable Y	A	B	Total
1	20	30	50
2	23	35	58
3	57	35	92
Total	100	100	200

a. What is the observed chi-square value?

_____

b. How many degrees of freedom do you have?

_____

c. What is the critical chi-square value?

_____

d. Are variables X and Y statistically independent? Why or why not?

_____

_____

_____

e. Calculate and interpret phi (φ).

_____

_____

_____

Exercise 13-8.   A major and continuing controversy in American politics has been the privatizing of governmental functions. Some states, for example, have turned to private contractors to house and rehabilitate their prisoners. Advocates claim that this practice saves the taxpayers money. Critics, however, say that these institutions, which are run on a for-profit basis, cut corners in inmate care and supervision.

Your employer, a nonprofit criminal justice organization, has funded a study of the issue. A small part of the resulting data appears in table 13-5. Your boss asks you to make sense of these numbers. This portion of the analysis involves two variables collected by the Bureau of Justice Statistics: (1) the operator of the facility, a federal or state agency or a private corporation, and (2) answers to the following question asked of supervisors: "Between July 1, 1994, and June 30, 1995, how many total inmates died while under the jurisdiction of this facility?"

TABLE 13-5 ■ Inmate Deaths by Facility

Type of Facility	Mean	Number of Institutions
Federal	8.86	(112)
State	19.48	(1,225)
Private	4.65	(110)
Total	17.53	(1,447)

Source	Sum of Squares	Degrees of Freedom	Mean Square	Observed F	Probability
Explained (type of prison)	31,341.430	2	15,670.715	7.490	.0006
Error	3,020,990.558	1,444	2,092.099		
Total	3,052,331.988	1,446			

Source: Table drawn using data from U.S. Bureau of Justice Statistics, "Correctional Populations in the United States, 1995," https://www.bjs.gov/index.cfm?ty=pbdetail&iid=744.

a. What type of analysis is this? Regression, analysis of variance, or something else?

_____

b. Given your answer to question (a), what is the objective of this analysis?

_____

_____

c. Did type of the facility (federal, state, private) have an effect on death rates among inmates? Explain.

_____

_____

d. Look at the data in both tables. Can you translate the problem into a statistical hypothesis? Explain it to your employer.

_____

_____

e. Assuming these data came from a random sample of prisons in the United States (they did not), could the differences between the death rates be attributable to sampling error, or is there evidence that the type of operator has an effect on mortality? Explain your answer. (*Hint:* This is a question of statistics, not substance.)

_____

_____

f. Interpret these data and statistical results substantively—that is, in a way that makes sense to journalists and public officials. Try to think of a reason why the statistical results reported in item e came out as they did. Are we observing a direct connection between type of prison and inmate death rates, or are there other variables that ought to be taken into account? Does the study shed any light on the policy debate about privatization?

_____

_____

_____

_____

Exercise 13-9. In this exercise you will have a computer generate a cross-tabulation and a chi-square statistic to match with your hand calculation. The first step is to open the "Individual Interest" file available on the *PSRM* student Web site using the statistical package recommended by your instructor. For this assignment you will be using the variables *Interest Politics News* (4 = very interested, 3 = somewhat interested, 2 = not too interested, 1= not at all interested) and *Female* (1 = female and 0 = not female).

a. Use your statistical package to create a cross-tabulation using the selected variables and to calculate chi-square. Attach the table you generate.

b. Using the cross-tabulation you generated, calculate chi-square by hand. The result should match the answer from your statistical package. Show your work below.

_____

_____

_____

_____

_____

_____

Exercise 13-10. In this exercise you will use an F-test to test a hypothesis that population means are equal using the hypothetical data in table 13-6. This table reports the number of political yard signs placed in yards by Democrats, Republicans, and independents. In this exercise we want to test the null hypothesis that the population means are equal using an F-test. Answer the questions below. (*Hint:* The textbook features step-by-step instructions for how to calculate sums of squares.)

TABLE 13-6 ■ Number of Political Yard Signs Planted by Party ID		
Number of Political Yard Signs (X)		
Democrats	**Republicans**	**Independents**
0	0	0
2	0	0
3	4	1
5	6	3
7	9	4

a. Calculate the between, within, and total degrees of freedom. Label each.

b. Calculate the between sum of squares.

c. Calculate the within sum of squares.

d. Calculate the total sum of squares.

e. Calculate F.

f. Find the F-critical score in appendix D in the textbook for a 95 percent confidence level (alpha = .05).

g. Are the population means statistically significantly different? How do you know?

Exercise 13-11. In this exercise you will focus on interpretation rather than calculation. Multivariate analysis simply means the simultaneous examination of three or more variables. With categorical data, researchers can analyze contingency tables. The examination of multiway contingency tables consists of three steps:

Step 1: Examine the relationship between the independent and dependent variables in a bivariate or two-way table. You might ask yourself, how strong is the relationship? Or, how are the individual categories related? Call this the *original relationship*. Take a look at table 13-7 to see the relationship between party support in 2017 in the UK by gender.

TABLE 13-7 ■ Original Relationship: Party Support by Gender		
Party	**Male**	**Female**
Conservative	2,653 (66%)	3,025 (63%)
Labour	1,357 (34%)	1,776 (37%)
Total	4,010 (100%)	4,801 (100%)
Chi-square = 9.47		
Gamma = 0.07		
Kendall's tau-b = 0.03		
Somers' D = 0.03		

Source: YouGov Survey Results, April 2–20, 2017, https://d25d2506sfb94s.cloudfront.net/cumulus_uploads/document/pvsh4yddit/InternalResults_170420_Demographics_W.pdf.

Note: Cells contain raw data count with percentages in parentheses.

Step 2: Having examined the relationship between voting intention and gender, we can now move on to the introduction of a third variable: age. Table 13-8 divides the sample not only by gender but also by whether the respondent is under forty or forty and over, creating two strata in each subtable (subtable A includes those under forty and subtable B includes those forty and over). You can now analyze the two variables within each stratum of a control variable. That is, you will have a two-way table (subtable A and subtable B) for each level of the control variable (age). Call this complex table the *controlled relationship*.

TABLE 13-8 ■ Controlled Relationship: Party Support by Gender by Age				
	Subtable A: Under 40		Subtable B: 40 and Over	
Party	Male	Female	Male	Female
Conservative	617 (49%)	642 (39%)	2,006 (72%)	2,225 (72%)
Labour	637 (51%)	999 (61%)	794 (28%)	882 (28%)
	1,254 (100%)	1,641 (100%)	2,800 (100%)	3,107 (100%)
	Chi-square = 29.39 Gamma = 0.20 Kendall's tau-b = 0.10 Somers' D = 0.10		Chi-square = 0.00 Gamma = 0.00 Kendall's tau-b = 0.00 Somers' D = 0.00	

Source: Author's calculations based on data from YouGov Survey Results, April 2–20, 2017, https://d25d2506sfb94s.cloudfront.net/cumulus_uploads/document/pvsh4yddit/InternalResults_170420_Demographics_W.pdf.

Note: Cells contain raw data count with percentages in parentheses.

Step 3: Draw a conclusion. If the original relationship remains more or less the same in each level of the control variable, then the control variable does not have an impact. If you observe a change in at least one of the subtables, then further analysis is necessary to determine how the control variable is affecting the relationship. If the original relationship is weaker (or disappears) in most of the subtables, you would have reason to suspect a spurious association.

Now that you understand tables 13-7 and 13-8, you are ready to try interpreting the results. Is there a relationship between party support and gender? Is age an important control variable? Answer the following questions to come to a conclusion:

a. Looking at table 13-7 first, what is the chi-square value?

_____

b. How many degrees of freedom do you have in table 13-7?

_____

c. What is the critical chi-square value (one-tailed, .05 level)? Use appendix C in the text to find this value.

_____

d. By comparing the observed chi-square value with the critical value, you can determine if the voting intention and gender variables are statistically independent. Are the variables statistically independent or related?

_____

e. What is the relationship between party support and gender in table 13-7? Use your answers about statistical independence above, along with cell percentages and the included measures of association, in making your conclusions.

_____

_____

_____

_____

_____

_____

f. Turning to table 13-8, are the variables in subtable A and subtable B statistically independent, or are they related? Use the same procedure you used in questions a-d to determine the answer.

_____

_____

_____

g. What is the relationship between party support and gender by age in table 13-8? Do you see a different relationship when controlling for age than you did when *not* controlling for age, or is the relationship unchanged? Use your answers about statistical independence above, along with cell percentages and the included measures of association, in making your conclusions.

_____

_____

_____

_____

_____

_____

14 REGRESSION

In chapter 14 of the textbook, we presented different forms of regression analysis, focusing on bivariate regression, multivariate regression, and logistic regression for use with a dichotomous dependent variable. Although some models and statistical procedures can get quite complicated, witht practice you will be able to use at least the simpler ones and to interpret their results. The exercises in this chapter give you practice in deciding which procedure is appropriate to use, how to relate your data to the procedure, and how to interpret the results of the analyses. Bivariate regression is a good starting point to explore regression because you can calculate a bivariate regression with simple arithmetic. Learning to calculate regressions by hand provides a feel for how regression works and how you can use it in an analysis.

Exercise 14-1. Chapter 14 introduced a number of analytical methods with similar-sounding names and potentially confusing terms. For each pair of words below, provide a definition for each word and explain the difference between the two.

a. Bivariate regression and multivariate regression

_____

_____

_____

b. Regression coefficient and regression constant

_____

_____

_____

c. Linear regression and logistic regression analysis

_____

_____

_____

d. Pearson's r and R^2

_____

_____

_____

Exercise 14-2.   At the heart of a regression analysis is the concept of minimizing the squared errors. Using figures 14-2, 14-3, and 14-4 in the textbook and the associated discussion, answer the following questions:

a.   Explain in plain English how a regression minimizes the squared errors. Why does a regression give us a single line that best fits the data?

_____

_____

_____

_____

b.   What is the difference between an observed value of the dependent variable (Y) and a predicted value of the dependent variable ($\hat{Y}$)?

_____

_____

_____

_____

c.   Why would one expect to see all of the data points on the line representing the regression line if an independent variable perfectly predicts a dependent variable?

_____

_____

_____

_____

Exercise 14-3.   Use the hypothetical data in table 14-1, where *Counties in State* is the independent variable and *Constituent Services Offices* is the dependent variable, to plot a regression line. Remember that in order to plot a regression line you will first need to perform all of the underlying calculations to find *b, a,* and $\hat{Y}$.

TABLE 14-1 ■ Exposure to and Sharing of Political Information		
State	**Counties in State**	**Constituent Services Offices**
Arizona	15	7
Connecticut	8	4
Delaware	3	2
Hawaii	5	2
Maine	16	8
Massachusetts	14	9
Nevada	16	6
New Hampshire	10	5
Rhode Island	5	2
Vermont	14	7

a. What is the slope?

_____

b. What is the intercept?

_____

c. Plot the regression line and include your calculations in the space below.

Exercise 14-4.   Define each of the following and explain its role in an analysis of a bivariate relationship:

a. R^2

_____

_____

_____

b. r

_____

_____

_____

c. $\hat{Y}$

_____

_____

_____

d. Y_i

_____

_____

_____

e. a

_____

_____

_____

f. b

_____

_____

_____

g. ε

_____

_____

_____

Exercise 14-5.   In this exercise you will use the "Human Development Index" data set available on the _PSRM_ Web site to test the relationship between life expectancy and education. Open the data file in the statistical package identified by your instructor. You will test the relationship between the variables _life expectancy_ (independent variable) and _mean years schooling_ (dependent variable) in a bivariate regression to answer the questions below.

a. Write a testable hypothesis about the relationship between life expectancy and mean years schooling. Make sure to include both a null and alternative hypothesis.

_____

b. Enter the variables in your statistical package and run an ordinary least squares regression. Attach the output to this exercise.

_____

c. Interpret the coefficient (the slope) in the context of your hypothesis.

_____

d. Decide whether you accept the null or alternative hypothesis with consideration of both substantive and statistical significance using a one-tailed test with 95 percent confidence.

_____

_____

e. Which statistics did you use to make your conclusion in item d? How did you determine statistical significance?

_____

_____

Exercise 14-6.   In this exercise you will use a regression to predict the vote percentage for Donald Trump in each state in the 2016 presidential election. To do this you will use the "States" data file available on the *PSRM* Web site. You will be testing the hypothesis that more voters identifying as conservative in a state led to a higher percentage of votes for Donald Trump. To test the relationship you should use the *conservative* and *Trump Vote Percentage* variables in an ordinary least squares regression in the statistical package your instructor has chosen. Answer the questions below.

a. Prepare a scatterplot of the percentage of votes for Trump (Y) against the number of conservative voters. Attach it to the assignment. Can you discern a relationship?

_____

_____

b. Compute Pearson's r, the correlation coefficient. What does it tell you about conservative voters and the percentage vote for Trump?

_____

_____

c. Use the statistical package to run an ordinary least squares regression with *conservative* as the independent variable and *Trump Vote Percentage* as the dependent variable. What is the estimated regression equation?

_____

_____

d. Interpret the regression coefficient statistically and substantively.

_____

_____

e. Is the regression coefficient statistically significant? Explain how you came to a decision on statistical significance.

_____

_____

Exercise 14-7.   *Suppose that you are a research assistant for a political science professor. The professor is working on a research project on immigration. The professor has asked you to examine the regression results in table 14-2 and answer the questions that follow.*

TABLE 14-2 ■ Regression Analysis of Immigration on Foreign-Born Population, 2016	
	Estimated Constant and Coefficient (standard error)
Constant	13,158.87
	(15,313.1)
Growth in GDP	0.0709
	(0.0046)

Source: Eurostat data available at https://ec.europa.eu/eurostat/en/web/products-datasets/-/TPS00176 and https://ec.europa.eu/eurostat/en/web/products-datasets/-/TPS00178, 2007.

Note: $N = 32$, $R^2 = .89$.

a. Compute the observed t for the regression coefficient.

_____

_____

b. What are the degrees of freedom for testing the significance of the regression coefficient?

_____

_____

c. What is the critical t at the .01 level for a one-tailed test?

_____

_____

d. Is the relationship between the independent and dependent variable statistically significant? How do you know?

_____

_____

e. Do you accept or reject the hypothesis that countries with larger foreign-born populations attract more immigration?

_____

_____

f. What percentage of the variation in immigration is "explained" by variation in foreign-born population?

_____

_____

g. What is the correlation between immigration and foreign-born population? How did you calculate Pearson's *r*?

_____

_____

Exercise 14-8.   Here are a few research hypotheses and designs. For each, explain what would be an appropriate tool for statistical analysis with multiple independent variables and why. (*Hint:* What are the dependent and independent variables, and how are they measured?) Choose among multivariate cross-tabulation, multivariate regression, and logistic regression.

a. An investigator believes acts of terrorism are caused mainly by sudden decreases in the economic standard of living of large numbers of society members. Data collected from fifty-five nations consist of the occurrence of an act of terror in a given year (yes or no) and measures of changes in income, poverty, employment, and manufacturing and agricultural output for the previous year.

_____

_____

_____

_____

b. A social scientist wonders whether the Sunbelt states are as politically conservative as they are reputed to be. She believes that, apart from perhaps social issues, the opinions and beliefs of people in different regions are roughly the same. Moreover, she thinks that any variation among regions stems mainly from differences in the social class composition of the citizens living in those places. She is analyzing an American National Election Study data file that includes categorical measures of region, attitudes on economic issues, and demographic characteristics, such as income, education, and ethnicity. What would be a good way to explore her hypothesis with these data?

_____

_____

_____

_____

c. A Washington think tank wants to know why some states have more generous health care benefits for the poor than others. Its members hypothesize that two general factors explain the difference: a state's overall political philosophy (degree of liberalism, for example) and economic capacity. The more liberal and wealthy a state, the more generous its health programs. The group's research firm has numerical indicators of health spending per capita for the poor, state ideology, percentage voting Democratic in national and state elections for the past ten years, per capita income, and economic growth over the past year. What method do you suggest the think tank use to test its hypothesis?

_____

_____

_____

_____

HELPFUL HINTS
INTERPRETING REGRESSION RESULTS

Here's a useful trick for understanding both the statistical and the substantive meaning of the coefficients of regression analysis. First, keep in mind the meaning of a multiple regression coefficient: It measures the amount the dependent variable Y changes for a one-unit change in a particular independent variable when all other independent variables have been held constant. This somewhat abstract definition can be made more meaningful when reading research results by following these steps:

1. Examine the summary table. For example, suppose, as is commonly the case, the findings are presented in a table like this:

Effects of Education and Race on Trust in the Judicial System

Variable	Coefficient
Constant	20***
Education (in years), X_1	2.0**
White (1 for white, 0 for not white), X_2	3.0**

Notes: $R^2 = .45$; ***$p < .001$, **$p < .01$.

Here the dependent variable (Y) is a scale of trust in the judicial system; the higher the score, the greater the trust. There are two independent variables, education and race, with the latter coded as a dummy variable (1 for whites, 0 for nonwhites).

2. Write the regression coefficients, including the constant if there is one, as an equation. Place the numeric values of the coefficients in an equation.

$$\hat{Y} = 20 + 2.0(Education) + 3.0(White)$$

Notice that we have included the constant term (20) and a plus sign before the coefficient for white. It is essential to keep track of the signs of the coefficients.

3. Imagine that the value of all independent variables is 0. Substitute this value into the equation. Example:

$$\hat{Y} = 20 + 2.0(0) + 3.0(0)$$
$$\hat{Y} = 20$$

What does that mean? If a person had no schooling ($X_1 = 0$) and was not white ($X_2 = 0$), the predicted level of trust ($\hat{Y}$) would be 20 units.

4. Now imagine that a person with no education ($X_1 = 0$) becomes white. Notice X_1 stays constant (that is, education is the same as in the previous equation) and X_2 changes, from 0 to 1. Place these new values in the equation and simplify.

$$\hat{Y} = 20 + 2.0(0) + 3.0(1)$$
$$\hat{Y} = 20 + 0 + 3$$
$$\hat{Y} = 23$$

This result clearly demonstrates that white—when education is held constant—"causes" or is associated with a three-unit increase in trust of the judicial system.

5. Now make another substitution. Go back to not white ($X_2 = 0$) and assume education increases by one year.

$$\hat{Y} = 20 + 2.0(1) + 3.0(0)$$
$$\hat{Y} = 20 + 2 + 0$$
$$\hat{Y} = 22$$

We see that an additional year of education increases trust among nonwhites by two units.

6. Make additional substitutions until you have a feel for the impact of the variables. Suppose, for instance, a white individual has twelve years of education. What is her predicted trust score?

$$\hat{Y} = 20 + 2.0(12) + 3.0(1)$$
$$\hat{Y} = 20 + 24 + 3$$
$$\hat{Y} = 47$$

7. After making these kinds of changes, you should be able to write a substantive summary of the regression model. In this case it appears that as people acquire more education, they have more trust in the court system. This is true of both whites and nonwhites. But for a given level of education, trust among nonwhites is lower than among whites. Your next step would be to expand on this conclusion. You might hypothesize that both poorly educated people and members of minority groups have different experiences in the criminal justice system. Of course, that argument goes beyond the data presented here.

8. The estimated coefficients are the heart and soul of the research. The information at the bottom of the table—and this format is typical of published articles—shows how well the data fit the linear regression model. The multiple regression coefficient, R^2, indicates that about half of the observed variation in trust scores is "explained" by education and race. The asterisks beside the coefficients indicate the level of significance. All three estimates are statistically significant—one at the .001 level, the others at the .01 level. (It is common for the coefficients in a model to have different degrees of significance.)

Exercise 14-9. Assume that two factors explain the number of representatives in national assemblies: population size and geographic size. Use the following regression coefficient values in table 14-3 to answer the question below. Population is measured in millions and geographic size is measured in square miles.

TABLE 14-3

Variable	Coefficient
Constant	100*
Population (in millions), X_1	5*
Geographic size (in millions of square miles), X_2	42*

Note: *$p < .01$

a. In which of the following countries would assembly membership be predicted to be highest? Why? (*Hint:* Use the least squares equation to predict assembly membership.) What are the predicted values for each country?

Country 1: population = 300; geographic size = 1.8

Country 2: population = 85; geographic size = 0.6

_____

_____

_____

_____

Exercise 14-10. Table 14-4 contains the results of a multiple regression analysis of the effects of development status (X_1), GNP (X_2), and infant mortality rates (deaths per 1,000 live births; X_3) on an indicator of political freedom, voice, and accountability (Y). The status variable is an indicator, or dummy variable, that is coded 0 for developed nations and 1 for developing nations. The dependent variable measures "the extent to which a country's citizens are able to participate in selecting their government, as well as freedom of expression, freedom of association, and free media. The index is scaled so that the mean of all scores is 0 and the standard deviation is 1.0. The higher the score, the greater the freedom."[1] The observed range is 3.32 (from −1.870 to 1.450).

TABLE 14-4 ■ Voice and Accountability Regressed on Development Status, GNP, and Infant Mortality				
Variable	Coefficient (standard error)	Mean	Observed Minimum	Observed Maximum
Constant	.9533			
	(.3415)			
Status	−1.4558	.5278	0	1
	(.3270)			
GNP	.00000798	18,450	600	68,800
	(.00000925)			
Infant mortality	−.00145	29.44	2	118
	(.002843)			

Source: Daniel Kaufmann, Aart Kraay, and Massimo Mastruzzi, "Aggregate and Individual Governance Indicators for 1996–2005," World Bank Policy Research Working Paper 4012, September 2006, http://info.worldbank.org/governance/wgi/pdf/GovernanceMattersVII.pdf.

a.   What is the estimated regression model?

_____

_____

_____

b.   Interpret the coefficient for status (X_1). Do not provide a mechanical answer. Instead, try to explain in terms an informed nonstatistician could understand.

_____

_____

_____

Exercise 14-11.   Political scientist Paul Goren investigated the relationship between core values and beliefs and policy preferences.[2] Goren defined *core beliefs* as "general descriptive beliefs about human nature and society in matters of public affairs,"[3] while *core values* are "evaluative standards citizens use to judge alternative social and political arrangements."[4] He wanted to know if, how, and under what conditions these perceptions and attitudes affect opinions on public policy, such as governmental welfare programs. Table 14-5 contains a small portion of his research results.

TABLE 14-5 ■ Social Welfare Policy Opposition Regressed on Eight Independent Variables

Variable	Coefficient	(Standard Error)
Constant	11.99	(.98)
Race	−1.57	(.45)
Gender	−.76	(.30)
Family income quartile	.03	(.14)
Party identification	.43	(.14)
Feelings toward beneficiaries	−.03	(.00)
Economic individualism	.20	(.04)
Equal opportunity opposition	.58	(.06)
Political expertise	.03	(.07)

$R^2 = .48$; $F_{9,637}$; $df = 73.42$; $N = 638$

Source: Paul Goren, "Core Principles and Policy Reasoning in Mass Publics: A Test of Two Theories," *British Journal of Political Science* 31(January 2001): 159–77, table 2.

The variables are as follows:

- Dependent variable, *Y:* Opposition to government social welfare provision. Additive, 25-point scale for which higher scores indicate greater opposition to governmental welfare services and spending.

- Independent variables, *Xk:*

  ☐ X_1: Race. 0 if white, 1 if African American

  ☐ X_2: Gender. 0 if male, 1 if female

☐ X_3: Income. Family income quartile (1–4)

☐ X_4: Party identification. 7-point scale: 0 for strong Democrat, 1 for Democrat, 2 for independent-leaning Democrat, 3 for independent, 4 for independent-leaning Republican, 5 for Republican, and 6 for strong Republican

☐ X_5: Feelings toward beneficiaries. Summation of thermometer scores of feelings toward blacks, poor people, and people on welfare. The higher the score, the warmer the feelings.

☐ X_6: Economic individualism. Scale of belief that "hard work pays off." 25-point additive scale with high scores indicating that being industrious, responsible, and self-reliant leads to economic success.

☐ X_7: Equal opportunity opposition. Belief "that society should do what is necessary to ensure that everyone has the same chance to get ahead in life."[5] 13-point additive scale with higher scores indicating increased opposition to efforts to promote equality.

☐ X_8: Political expertise. 0–8 scale of factual political knowledge with higher scores indicating more information and "sophistication."[6]

a. What kind of variable is gender? _____

b. Write out the regression equation for this model.

_____

_____

c. Provide a short verbal interpretation of the regression coefficient for income (X_3). Assume you are explaining to someone who is familiar with political science but not with multiple regression.

_____

_____

_____

_____

d. Give a substantive interpretation or explanation of the coefficient for gender (X_2).

_____

_____

_____

e. If all of the independent variables have scores of 0, what is the predicted value of the dependent variable?

_____

f. Can you offer a substantive interpretation of your answer to part e? That is, explain its meaning to a politician.

_____

_____

_____

_____

g. What is the numerical effect of being African American ($X_1 = 1$) and in the third quartile of income ($X_4 = 3$) if all other variables have scores of 0?

_____

h. Consider an African American female (that is, $X_1 = 1$ and $X_2 = 1$) with an expertise score of $X_8 = 2.87$. Assume all the other variables are 0. What is the predicted opposition scale score?

_____

i. The author of this study reports that the average score for economic individualism (X_6) is 13.70 and the mean for equal opportunity opposition (X_7) is 3.53.[7] Consider an African American female independent (that is, $X_4 = 3$) with an expertise score (X_8) of 2.57 and in the second quartile of income ($X_3 = 2$). Assume the score on feelings toward beneficiaries (X_5) = 50. If this person has average scores on individualism and equal opportunity opposition, what would be her predicted score on opposition to social welfare?

_____

_____

_____

j. Suppose this same individual switches to strong Democrat from independent but retains the same characteristics (measures) on all the other variables in the previous question. What is the effect of this change in party identification? _____
What is her predicted value on Y, social welfare policy opposition? _____

k. Given the N in the table, what is the appropriate sampling distribution to test the significance of individual coefficients?

_____

l. The standard errors for the coefficients appear in table 14-5. What is the observed test statistic for gender? Is it statistically significant at the .05 level? At the .01 level? (Use a two-tailed test for both tests.)

_____

m. What is the observed test statistic for political expertise (X_8)? Is it statistically significant at the .05 level? At the .01 level? (Use a one-tailed test.)

_____

n. What does the R^2 tell you about the fit of the data to the model?

_____

Exercise 14-12. Imagine that you and your lab partner are working on a lab assignment in which you must use a bivariate regression to test hypotheses about support for the president. You are interested in testing a hypothesis about religion. Your lab partner is concerned about using religion as an independent variable in a regression because the available religion variable from the 2016 American National Election Study is a nominal variable (see figure 14-1) and your professor told you that nominal variables with multiple categories cannot be used in regression. Is your friend correct to be concerned? Is there any way you can recode or manipulate this variable for use as an independent variable?

FIGURE 14-1 ■ Nominal Level Measure of Religion

Do you consider yourself Protestant, Roman Catholic, Jewish, or something else?[8]

1. Protestant

2. Catholic

3. Jewish

4. Other

_____

_____

_____

_____

Exercise 14-13. Multiple regression offers the opportunity to test whether the relationship between variables holds up in the presence of control variables. Consider, for example, the relationship between the percentage of children ages 0–18 in a state and the percentage vote for Donald Trump in each state in 2016. Open the "States" data file available on the *PSRM* Web site using the statistical package chosen by your instructor and answer the questions below. Use a two-tailed test and a 95 percent confidence level when assessing statistical significance.

a. Run an ordinary least squares regression using the *children* variable as the independent variable and *Trump Vote Percentage* as the dependent variable. Attach your results. Interpret the relationship between the percentage of children in a state and the vote percentage for Donald Trump. Make sure you interpret the coefficient and statistical significance.

_____

_____

b. Why might this result be flawed? Is there substantive significance?

_____

_____

c. Run a second regression that adds another independent variable, *conservative*, that measures the percentage of conservative voters in each state. Attach your regression output. Interpret this regression, making sure to include a discussion of coefficients and statistical significance.

_____

_____

d. What happened to the relationship between *children* and *Trump Vote Percentage* when controlling for the percentage of conservatives in each state? Why do you think this happened?

_____

_____

_____

_____

Exercise 14-14. Continuing from exercise 14-13, examine additional variables in the "States" file that might predict Donald Trump's vote percentage in 2016. Select two more variables to add to the multiple regression you executed above with *children* and *conservative*.

a. What do you expect to see when you add your additional two variables?

_____

_____

b. Run your new regression with *children, conservative,* and two additional independent variables and *Trump Vote Percentage* as the dependent variable. Interpret the results, making sure to include a discussion of each coefficient and statistical significance.

_____

_____

_____

_____

c. Did you find any unexpected results?

_____

_____

HELPFUL HINTS
PREPARING AND ORGANIZING A MULTIVARIATE ANALYSIS

Analyzing more than two variables at a time can be a daunting chore, even for experienced data analysts. The secret, we believe, is the same as for any academic undertaking: Think before acting. In the case of multivariate analysis, careful planning is of utmost importance. Hence, we offer a few suggestions to help you organize your research:

- As we discussed in previous chapters of the textbook, it is essential that you state a few working hypotheses. If you sit in front of a computer before organizing your thoughts, you will soon be drowned in printout. We guarantee it.

- If you are given a data set, pick a likely dependent variable—something that might be important to understand or explain. Then ask yourself which of the other variables in the file might be related to it. If you

are starting from scratch, you have more leeway. But in any case, try to convert these ideas into substantive hypotheses. Remember, a hypothesis is a tentative statement subject to verification. The result of the test is less important than starting with a meaningful proposition. Why? Because whether one accepts or rejects it, something of value has been learned. Testing trivial propositions (for example, poverty among children is correlated with poverty among families) does not advance our knowledge of anything.

- Similarly, think carefully about what would be appropriate indicators of general explanatory factors. Suppose, for instance, you believe high crime rates encourage people to leave cities for the suburbs or countryside. If you are trying to explain migration to the suburbs, one of your independent variables would be

(Continued)

(Continued)

crime, which can be measured by, say, homicide rates or property lost to theft. Whatever the case, think of broad explanatory factors and empirical indicators of those factors.

- Sometimes the choice of variables is straightforward. Frequently, however, you may need your imagination to construct indicators. Suppose you theorize that changes in population density explain something, but the data at your disposal contain only the actual populations and areas of cities for 1994 and 2004. You first need to compute a density for each year by dividing total population by area to obtain, say, persons per square mile. Then you could calculate another indicator, "percentage change in population density from 1994 to 2004." Most software programs make these sorts of transformations easy.

- Remember that the data are empirical indicators of underlying theoretical concepts. You cannot expect them to be perfectly or even strongly related to the dependent variable or to one another. In general, if you find a model that explains 40 to 50 percent of the statistical variation in the dependent variable, you will be doing well.

- We strongly urge you to analyze each variable individually, especially the dependent variable, before moving on to analyzing relationships between variables. Use the methods described in chapter 11 of the textbook.

- If your analysis involves multiple regression, first obtain plots of all the variables against each other. Doing so will reveal important aspects of the relationships, such as curvilinearity, the existence of outlying points, and the lack of variation in one or both variables. All these aspects can and should be taken into consideration.

- Outliers can present serious problems in multivariate analysis. Simply deleting the outliers, however, is typically not a good idea. But it is permissible, even advisable in some instances, to delete the outlying cases if you can do so on substantive grounds. Perhaps there is something about that particular case that makes it unsuitable for inclusion in a sample. Another solution is to transform variables. Taking the log of a variable can mitigate the effects of a few very large numbers on a statistical procedure. Another option is to include the outlier and explain how its inclusion in the analysis changes the results. Regardless of how you deal with outliers, be sure to describe your methods in your report so the reader can make a fully informed judgment on the results and conclusions.

- It helps to obtain a correlation matrix of your variables. This table will point to variables that are not related to much of anything and that might be dropped from the analysis. Equally important, correlation coefficients will help you decide whether an independent variable is related in the way your hypothesis predicts. If there should be a negative relationship, for instance, and the correlation is positive, your starting assumption may be wrong or you may have to look more carefully at the variable's definition.

- A correlation and a plot can also flag another possible problem. Sometimes two independent variables are so highly correlated that they are practically equivalent to each other. In this case, choose one of the variables for inclusion and eliminate the other.

- Your final regression model may be much simpler than your initial expectations. That is probably a good thing because the goal of science is to find the simplest equation that has the highest predictive capacity. It is not important to include lots and lots of variables. One technique is to add or subtract one variable at a time and determine if it appreciably changes the model. You may be able to eliminate quite a few variables this way, thereby reducing complexity.

Exercise 14-15.   Dummy variables are an important type of variable in statistical analysis. Answer each of the following questions about dummy variables:

a.   Define a dummy variable.

_____

_____

b.   Why is a dummy variable typically assigned the values of 1 and 0?

_____

_____

c. How can a dummy variable be used to convert a categorical variable into a variable that can be used in higher-order statistical analyses? Provide an example of a categorical variable with a nominal level of measurement and explain how it could be transformed into at least one dummy variable.

_____

_____

_____

_____

Exercise 14-16.   Open the "Social Vote" data set available on the *PSRM* Web site in the statistical package chosen by your instructor. Find the *Shared Information* variable, which indicates whether the respondent encouraged anyone to vote for Barack Obama or Mitt Romney by posting on a social networking site, such as Facebook or Twitter, in the last thirty days. Select the cases where *Shared Information* equals 1 or 0 and delete the other cases. Then, choose two variables that you think explain why individuals would use social media to ask others to vote for a candidate and include all three variables in a logistic regression model. Attach your results and interpret the results below. Make sure to interpret as much as you can about the coefficients and the model as a whole.

_____

_____

_____

_____

_____

_____

_____

_____

NOTES

1. Daniel Kaufmann, Aart Kraay, and Massimo Mastruzzi, "Aggregate and Individual Governance Indicators for 1996–2005," World Bank Policy Research Working Paper 4012, September 2006, http://info.worldbank.org/governance/wgi/pdf/GovernanceMattersVII.pdf.

2. Paul Goren, "Core Principles and Policy Reasoning in Mass Publics: A Test of Two Theories," *British Journal of Political Science* 31(January 2001): 159–77. The coefficients used in this assignment differ from those in the published table. The changes were made after personal communication with the author.

3. Ibid., 160.

4. Ibid., 160–61.

5. Ibid., 165.

6. Ibid., 164–66.

7. Ibid., 176, table A.

8. The 2016 American National Election Study pretest questionnaire is available at https://www.electionstudies.org/wp-content/uploads/2018/03/anes_timeseries_2016_qnaire_pre.pdf.